The Music of the Streets

Also by Michael Robinson and published by Ginninderra Press
The Tiger in the Vineyard

Michael Robinson

The Music of the Streets

Acknowledgements

Poems in this collection have appeared in the following journals:
Poetry Matters, Studio, Uneven Floor.

Preparation of this book was supported by a grant from the Western Australian Department of Culture and the Arts.

Government of **Western Australia**
Department of **Culture and the Arts**

The Music of the Streets
ISBN 978 1 76041 427 6
Copyright © text Michael Robinson 2017
Cover: Jacqui Telford

First published 2017 by
GINNINDERRA PRESS
PO Box 3461 Port Adelaide 5015 Australia
www.ginninderrapress.com.au

Contents

Preface	9
Theme	16

I The vacancy and the fire — 17

Letter to the Minister	19
The Mural	20
The Collision	22
'I Sell Love'	25
Sleeping Rough	26
The Therapist and the Sea	27
To the Fourth Generation	28
Anaesthesia	30
Child of Privilege	32
The Waiting Room	33
Graduation Day	35
The Bookshop	37
The Youth Worker and the Machete	38

II Dancing with children's names — 43

The Robbers	45
Five Witnesses	47
The Hospital	52
The Rope	54
Reunion	56
The Answer	58
Seven Silent Women	59
In a Mist	62
The Horses of Achilles	64
Persephone at Admissions	67

III Sketches from the front line	71
Sketches from the front line	73
IV Soldiers of compassion	77
Homage to an Outreach Worker	79
Homage to a Midwife	82
Homage to a Youth Worker	85
The Anniversary	89
V Hymning the sun	91
The Grieving Stone	93
The Power to Lie	94
The Evaluator	95
The Music of the Streets	99
The Reception	103
Mission Statement	106
The Flood	107
The Ark	108
The Rain-tree and the Fire-tree	110
VI A tapestry of murder	115
A Handful of Diamonds	117
Graffiti Artist	119
Seasons of Mortality	121
Death of a Novelist	123
The Three Gardens	125
Father and Child	127

VII A young and troubled century	129
The Pioneers' Dream	131
In the Cathedral of the Homeless	136
Easter Saturday	139
Saturday Evening, Sunday Morning	142
VIII The last judgement	145
The Last Judgement of the Homeless	147

Preface

I am grateful to all the young people, service providers, friends and colleagues who have shared their experiences and enlightened and enriched me over the years. Special thanks go to Narell Black, Rona Chadwick, Katie Culkin, Gary Partington, Chantal Roberts and Jacqui Telford.

Nonetheless, all and any opinions expressed or implied are entirely my own responsibility and no one else's. (Since some are in the voices of fictional characters, not all entirely admirable, they aren't all necessarily mine. But they are all my responsibility.)

From 1997 to 2010, I had the privilege of managing a funding program called Innovative Health Services for Homeless Youth (IHSHY), among other responsibilities, while working for the Western Australian Department of Health. During that time and subsequently, I have had the opportunity to meet and learn from numerous remarkable young people and numerous equally remarkable, and dedicated, service providers, in an area of work that has sadly not had a high political profile. But it's an area where lives are saved and transformed that would otherwise have been lost.

According to the Australian Bureau of Statistics, at the time of the 2011 census there were over 105,000 homeless people in Australia. Of these, 65% were aged under thirty-five (ABS, *Census of Population and Housing: Estimating Homelessness Australia*). The 2013–14 survey conducted by the Telethon Kids Institute in partnership with Roy Morgan Research found that one in seven children and young people experienced a mental disorder in the previous twelve months – the equivalent of 560,000 young Australians (Australian Government, *The Mental Health of Children and Adolescents: Report on the Second Australian Child and Adolescent Survey of Mental Health and Wellbeing*). An inquiry conducted in Western Australia found that one in six children and young people between the ages of four and seventeen years in that state experience a mental health problem (Commissioner for Children and Young People, *Report of the Inquiry into the mental health and wellbeing of children and young people in Western Australia*).

These — and there are many other indicators that could be cited — are signs that there is a substantial number of young people, and formerly young people, who are disadvantaged and disfranchised in what it is easy to think of as a prosperous society.

The causes of this are doubtless complex and don't fit easily into anyone's political agenda, either of the left or the right, having elements discordant to both. But recognising a problem is the first step to diagnosing and curing it and without recognition it will grow and get worse. Happily it has been shown that there are ways of helping and supporting young people that succeed — that can save lives and change them.

I'm grateful to the authors of several evaluations and other reports that dramatically confirmed the value of these services. They include, among others, a randomised controlled trial of the Adolescent Mothers Support Service that showed reduction in mortality and morbidity among children of adolescent mothers, and a reduction in the number of children taken into state care (Quinlivan, J.A., Box, H., and Evans, S.F., 'Postnatal home visits in teenage mothers: a randomised controlled trial,' *Lancet* 361 (2003), pages 893–900); a national review of IHSHY by Health Services International in 2007; the National Youth Commission report *Australia's Homeless Youth* (2008); *An evaluation of the accessibility and acceptability of the Innovative Health Services for Homeless Youth (IHSHY) Program in the Perth metropolitan area* (2011), by Tracy Reibel and Tanyana Jackiewicz of the Telethon Institute for Child Health Research, now the Telethon Kids Institute; and *Keeping Kids on Track: An initiative developing the resilience of Aboriginal students during a critical transition phase* (2012), a five-year National Health and Medical Research Council (NHMRC) funded research project based on the in-school Happy Kids model and led by Gary Partington, Karen Anderson and the late and much missed Ann Galloway of Edith Cowan University.

Thanks are also due, and given, to all my former colleagues in the Western Australian Department of Health and in federal, state and local governments more broadly who participated in and supported this work with homeless and at risk young people. They might not all find it helpful if I were to name them, but they know who they are. As do those who chose rather to hinder and to block these efforts.

The poems in this collection draw on my own and others' experiences. But – with the exception of certain entirely complimentary passages where service providers may and should recognise themselves – they are works of fiction and no reference to any living person is intended.

For the same reason, I have not offered an account of my personal experiences of trauma and violence. Inevitably they involve others, both living and dead, whose privacy I want to respect. A further reason is that I think it wrong to expect writers to present credentials drawn from their personal lives.

To adapt a phrase from Goethe, 'everything was lived, but not as it is written'.

'In a world in agreement with itself,' writes the twentieth-century French critic Albert Thibaudet, 'individuals would become a scandal, an infirmity of being. God has done well to choose a world of individuals.' Ours is decidedly not a world or time in agreement with itself. Those who suffer because of the time being out of joint are nonetheless individuals, and each has his or her infinite and irreplaceable value.

Poetry has been thought in the past to deal with generalities, with universals. But our knowledge of generalities can come only through knowledge (which itself must necessarily be incomplete) of individuals, including ourselves and our thoughts and experiences. And to project generalities, abstracted from incomplete knowledge of individuals, back onto other individuals is a sure cause of error. The more so as we ascend in complexity and self-awareness. One stone is much like another stone, though each has still its unique quality of what Duns Scotus calls *haecceitas*, 'thisness' – being this stone and no other. But no human being is quite like another.

(The opposite doctrine – put about by the young Ezra Pound among many others – that poetry must avoid abstractions and work only with the concrete particular errs for contrasting but related reasons. It's impossible to think about or describe any individual, any particular, without referring to properties, relations, notions of time and space – and our references to all of these, though not the things themselves, are themselves abstractions drawn from our own and others' past experiences, perceptions and reflections.)

So the uniqueness and dignity of the individual seems to me a central and unavoidable concern of poetry – not any the less when the individual is in difficult circumstances. And maybe more so when the difficult circumstances are the products of breakdowns in family, community, shared belief, education and conditions of employment whose costs are still not recognised.

Poetry must have its intrinsic value as poetry. Neither moral virtue nor social interest alone makes poetry, and still less does that very different thing, the feeling that one is virtuous. But language (certain distinguished voices to the contrary notwithstanding) is, though distinct from other things, not separate from them – from mind, spirit, nature and society. So there is no requirement, indeed there can't be a requirement, for poetry to be sundered from the world around it. Nor does language 'construct' these other things. Because it can indeed influence people's thoughts, its users have a responsibility to be sensitive and attentive in using it, as they must, to consider and describe the realities that comprise their subject matter.

But poetry, at least the kind of poetry I attempt here, aims to evoke and reflect, not to produce a documentary. There are those who would approach subject matter like this by portraying individuals stripped of dignity – in the manner, say, of Burroughs or Bukowski. Maybe such writing can be justified – up to a point – on grounds of satiric decorum, the theory of what style is proper to satire. But only up to a point. The temptation to write as though alcoholic vomit were the truest reality is evidently strong, and Burroughs could not reach what he called the Western Lands. There are older, deeper and stronger traditions that enable human dignity and the hope of redemption to be found in suffering and deprivation as much as in peace.

Reflecting contemporary realities need not mean accepting any particular contemporary attitudes or philosophies. Paradoxical as it may sound, it cannot and should not mean this, since many of the most grievous contemporary realities arise in part precisely from the inadequacy and wrongness of contemporary attitudes and philosophies.

People who are homeless or in prison, who have suffered abuse or violence, who are Indigenous or non-Indigenous, who are refugees or who are not refugees, who are privileged or not privileged (continue *ad libitum*), are first and foremost people. This is the limitation, and all too often the cruelty, of contemporary identity politics, however well-intentioned. The beginning of wisdom (as disability advocates used to remind us) is to see the person before the problems. Only in this way can you hope to see both the person and the problems.

Poems in this collection (or earlier drafts of them) have appeared in the following print and online journals: *Poetry Matters*, *Studio*, *Uneven Floor*. My particular thanks to Paul Grover, editor of *Studio*, for including substantial selections from my drafts for this book in the single-author edition given to my work, *Light's Horizon* (*Studio* 133, 2015).

Preparation of this book was supported by a grant from the Western Australian Department of Culture and the Arts.

His triumph was in the uprising of the fallen, and his joy was in the renewal of hope.
– Tolkien, *Morgoth's Ring*, 203

>   more able to endure,
> As more exposed to suffering and distress;
> Thence also, more alive to tenderness.

– Wordsworth, 'Character of the Happy Warrior,' 24–6

> There is no merit in the wise
> But Love, (the shepherds' sacrifice).
> Wise men, all ways of knowing past,
> To the shepherds' wonder come at last.

– Godolphin, 'Hymn,' 13–16

It is to be remembered, too, that there is not the same kind of correctness in poetry as in politics.
– Aristotle, *De Poetica*, 1460b14

Cognition of anything only by resemblances and by universals is not the most perfect and intuitive cognition of the thing itself.
– Duns Scotus, *Ordinatio*, Book I, Distinction 2, part 1, question 3, 167; *Opera Omnia* (Vatican edition) II, 227–8

When institutions are crumbling, when chaos surges at the gates, art can only record the event it has perhaps helped to bring on.
– William K. Wimsatt, *Day of the Leopards*, xii

Only in devastation does the negative will feel that it has reality.
– Hegel, *Philosophy of Right*, tr. S.W. Dyde, 14

The whole Earth cannot be in greater distress than *one* soul.
– Wittgenstein, *Culture and Value*, 52

Theme

Let others write of war and politics,
Field and farm smouldering, love's awkwardness,
Domestic infelicities, love's hidden chasms,
Flood pages with fantasised impossible sex,
Reprove, if they must, Aeneas and his Virgil,
Poet of civilisation and the refugee,
Fate's ruthlessness, unwilling sailors' gales,
Allusion to the monumental past,
Or linger on death and tawdry four-letter words,
Lament how their fathers failed to understand them.
My theme's atonement and the dispossessed,
Unacknowledged dignity of the stranger
Who limps from prison cell to cold pavement,
Refuge to makeshift shelter; memory
Of battles without parades, unchronicled heroes
Of survival's daily siege; betrayal and bravery
Without medals; death and the fires of resurrection.

I

The vacancy and the fire

Letter to the Minister

These things were forbidden me
By destiny's inscrutable government,
Cabinet decisions relayed
From a roofless, starless capital:

Satin, ripe fruit, safe nights,
A ceiling that doesn't drip,
Warm and familiar quilts,
Food on plates and linen,
Meat not tasting of cardboard,
Wounds only from the cricket field
Free to mend at leisure,
Pulse of bodies touching
In the slow work of love,
Green leaves and purple flowers
That play in the air like rain,
Revelation of crisp strawberries.

The Mural

He loved the night sky. Drinking with friends
On the sober, ageless beach, hurling beer cans
Into the choppy sea, he walked away,
Shoes crunching softly on the grey sand,
Past thickets of black grass where the road ends
And unseen marsupials rustle and play,
Lizards and whispering snakes, to stand
And look up alone at unreachable, free
Stars puzzlingly
Winking and burning in the riddling arches
Of impossible, high, soft blankness
Far from his world of theft, car chases,
Inarticulate unhappiness,
And think it would be good to be an astronaut
Exploring the vacancy and the fire.
He'd look down on the streets' trivial wars.
They'd fade into aquamarine and gold.
Drunkenness and brutal parents would grow old
And dwindle into untouchable points of thought,
Shivering like the galaxies.

                             When
He died, his friends remembered. They let stars
Pour icy rays of flame around the mural
They painted on a ruin, to recall
Something he had meant and lost.

                            The factory
Wall's chipped bricks chorused with memory

And love, wordless memory, wordless protest
At the broken tyranny of time, wordless mourning.
Dead roses lay in hills above a forest,
Green with fresh rain, newborn petals glowing.

Tipped with light, they hovered above a stream flowing
Around washed brown rocks. Waves combed from the west,
Where a troubled sea fell. Wild lilies curled
Over a shimmering port drowned among its lights,

Ships at anchor sleeping. On bushland heights
Planes opened fire-kissed wings and whirled,
Over lakes, sports grounds, offices. Sweet peas burned.
Pedestrians wandered in dreams' changeable flames.

Roads, cafés and rivers with no names
Sparked with a thousand years' colour. Almond blossoms turned

Gardens into wells of starlight, crowned bright leaves with white
Jewels of fire. Day ebbed into night,
Trucks' beams lined a streaked highway. The fine breath
Of strange stars touched scenes of secrecy and light.

In silence unfitting to the young
They carried his ashes to the shore.
And now he travels in leaves of ash that pass
Into the lapping, jumping tides,
Memory and the ruthless, many-shaded sea,
Under limestone cliffs and fierce grass.

The Collision

The two cars he shattered
In his and others' deaths
Lie in their marriage of ruin in a wrecker's yard –

One stolen
That helpless, fated night from a peaceful carport,
Student's treasure purchased steadily, patiently,
Hot-wired at midnight,

Engine that screamed in its last agony,

Another bought with love for a torn family,
Earned with weeks and years of mundane labour,
Patient days in a call centre.

Dissevered, deconstructed red nineties hatchback,
Modest, disunited grey sedan,
Twists of mudguards, punctured radiators, dislocated lamps,
Salvageable cylinder block and fractured doors.

Lethal child who was browbeaten, scarred with his century's brand,
Branded in the aftermath of birth, abandoned,
Borrowed, broken, finger-marked, returned,
Traded through courtrooms and detention centres,
Taught never to read,
Never to know carefree winters,
Lectured in shame.

Driver at a hundred and eighty kilometres an hour
Who fled from police and the ruthlessness of years
To a burning intersection with humanity.

Stars evoked the indifference of gardens,
Roses behind white fences cherished dew,
Flame trees cradled small hours in dark boughs.

The woman and her daughter
He met and didn't meet that drugged night
Lie together in death
As once in parturition, in a green avenue's
Delicacy of changeable morning and afternoon light,
Under sheltering, clashing
Leaves the wind explores.

White and sunlit presence of stones and soil,

Ground that somewhere gathers
The unknown soldier of the destined hour,
The wronged and killing stranger.

A bereaved father, a widower struggles to concentrate
On figures besieging an unforgivable screen,
Naked and afraid beneath the kindness of colleagues
On the twenty-second floor of a long purgatory.

A house rough with the repetitive shock
Of old, familiar things.

Fragile crosses by the cool pavement,
Silent, crying crosses and springing flowers.

And every Sunday morning at one a.m.
Fire and murder at the intersection
Replay themselves in shining mirrors of eternity.

Blaze of terror, police lights turning and flashing,
Futile ambulances mounted on the grass verge,
Traffic signals repeating their useless drumbeat.

Circles of mourning spread around the earth.

'I Sell Love'

My parents' names were rage and loneliness.
Determined I must stay out of the rain,
The faithless rain that splashed the edges of my mattress
In the alley behind the houses where I'd sleep
Under strange, black eaves, I walk the changing, deep
Patchwork of night, and earn my money from men
Who throw spare dollars into my wishing well,
To buy the hand of freedom I can sell.

I sell love. A moment's soft release
From the ache of solitude. The cars roll slow,
One stops. I sell kind conversation, ease,
Gentleness, the dawn of unknown beauty,
Freedom, my hand, music and ecstasy.
I've seen the shock of tenderness. I know
The young man in his meanness and the stray,
Exploratory fingers of the earth-bound grey.

I'm fifteen years old. Ground low in a mill
Clattering and pounding with fury and drunkenness,
I tried to bake fresh bread. I'm trying still.
Headlights rise and set behind the buildings.
Residents' laughter, their mockery that stings
Bewilder me. I sell my cheap caress.
I suffer the breaking of a society.
The songs of fallen angels comfort me.

Sleeping Rough

They say it's all her own fault. Smells
Of stale mattresses, crusts and urine smear
A squat without light, and stolen sanctity wells
From stained walls and damp blankets, where
She sleeps and wakes alone, without a voice.
All this, you might suppose, is her own choice.
Home, warmth, her family cast aside
For wantonness, laziness, youthful rage and pride.

Here but for heaven's grace walk you or I,
Whom fortune feeds or curses at its measure,
All of us who breathe under the sky,
Subject to father's rape or stranger's pleasure,
Shadows of love while nights teem and fly,
And children dream in ruins and cultures die.

The Therapist and the Sea

Near the mourning beach
Where palms catch the sea wind,
Throw it one to another
Like reckless children at play
In a game without rules or victory,

In a newly painted building,
On a street whose name I've forgotten,
The therapist said, 'And there's one
Child who's so damaged

'I take him for picnics on the beach,
Rides in the ferry,
Walks along the jetty,
Over the unforgettable sea
Chopped and broken by weeds
That wave in the current like hands,
Only to give him some pleasant
Memories in his night.'

Though you wake
In hell built by generations
Whose agony none can measure,
Let there be drops of grace
To cool your tongue: the sea,
Songs of a friendly voice,
Ships, a heron's flight,
Wings mending the sun.

To the Fourth Generation

Sharp, transparent water laps around
The savage rock that looms out of the sea
Like a temple built by mindless hands to thousand-
Year-old rituals, bloodstained sacrifice to the restless
Noise of the changing tides. The roadhouse lights
Float pale and yellow over the cooling bitumen
And the sun's red farewell darkens the ripples.
Tired after many hours'
Driving, many years'
Dying, choked in mists of wine, television,
Drugs, pornography, working girls, I leave
My dusty four-wheel drive in an angled bay
And sidle in.

      My son.
I hardly recognise you. Seated at a neighbouring
Table, your small, bewildered, hurt eyes,
Now, as I remember them, red-rimmed,
Narrow lips and high forehead the same.
You must be forty now. The strident decades,
Clouded by roads and confused memories
Pour over me again. My four children.
Three different mothers. A morass
Of child support, divorce, recrimination.
Outcrops of violence. My two daughters.
The other son I haven't seen since prison
Opened its gates and cast me out.

      Rasp and squeal
Of conversation breaks and falls around us. Chips grow cold.

And you've had four children, just as I did,
Each with a different mother. I glimpse the waves
Twinkling and rolling outside the soundless windows.

They haunt your dreams, your loved, forgotten boys,
Girls vanished into the city's maze of lightning
And secret storms. And now your elder son,
In an adult prison for selling methamphetamine,
Has two infant daughters by two young women, helpless
Hostages of the burning clouds, the fire.

                            I shake your hand,
Walk past my car and out onto the shadowy,
Grey, shining beach. The sea rustles,
Roars, whispers, curls, splashes.

                      My son.
My son. The fires flicker
In the silence behind my thoughts. The black grass
Smoulders. Like an accident victim
Abandoned centuries ago, to ache in the darkness
On a rainy highway, the streaming rock
Calls its pain to the uncomprehending wind.

Anaesthesia

'Don't.
Worry.
Because.
I.
Talk.
Slow.'

Said the paint sniffer to the young heroin user
From the peer support and outreach group
Who wanted to help him.

'This.
Is.
My.
Nor-
Mal.
Talk.'

The heroin user told this story
Over tea, cakes and coffee,
His face worn grey by hepatitis.
'I've lost more weight,' he said.
'I wish I could gain some.'

And in parks and taxis
Children hang cans of paint
Around their necks, or cover their glue
In plastic shopping bags,

Anaesthetising
(If you can pronounce it)
Inscrutable green grass,
Leaning offices, closed
Faces, memory of strangers,
Rumour of falling forests, morning's
Abuse, midday's shame.

Child of Privilege

He was born to graceful fortune.
Creative mystery drew him out of nowhere
And nothing and the forges beyond years
Where newness forms under the imperishable force
Of ageless art; bestowed upon him gifts,
A white mansion above a gliding park,
Green in the transient noon, or healed and washed
By clouds of rain. Four cars glistened in a swept
And shining car port. His was the blessing of history.
He was the child ardent daybreak welcomed
With deeper than human warmth.

                              Only not now.
Not now, when his father's drunk, unfocused rages,
Wounded roars of a bewildered animal
Goaded like a bull in the ring by the lances of chaos,
His mother's cocaine, her sequence of worsening lovers
Hollow the marble mansion to a black arena
Where polished stairways sweep through emptiness
Pinpricked by distant, tiny blades of starlight.

Not now, when tears and the breath of dust pursue him
To boarding school, where two searing bullies
Grasp his ankles and he swings head downward
From a third-storey window, and red bricks
And crumbling mortar sway before his eyes,
Dark grass beckons and netted leaves
Rise from icy branches in ashen crowns.

The Waiting Room

I grasp my child in tired hands. Only a few
Hours of daylight born, his clear eyes, new
To the world, survey my face. Calmly, methodically,
He searches left to right, left to right. Did he
Dream in the womb, then wake?
Light and dark, uncomprehended, break
And spread, reveal mother and father, nameless,
A hospital room, strange voices, and the endless,
Intricate labyrinths of a welcoming family.

His eyes observe the patterns of the nursery.
Images of other children, images of destiny
Burn on the walls like slow, terrible lightning.
Some will awake to narratives of tightening
Ignorance, rage and fear.
Shadows of arrest and violence draw near.
Barbed wire shines like platinum in the sunlight.
Clouds gather above buildings and ghosts fight,
Generations of dead forebears arguing.

Fog thickens over the park below us. Futures
Glow and fade in brief, dazzling pictures
That form and disperse on the magazine table.
Treasure squandered on racetrack and brothel,
Betrayal in the Family Court,
Enduring, sacrificial love cut short,
Shouts in warm twilight, percussion of glass breaking,
Bellows of blindness, lips and hands shaking.
Rays of eerie sun touch the hospital.

The walls display tomorrow's remorseless years.
A vision of a police van appears,
A young innocent standing in the dock,
Sketch of a broken body, a bloodstained rock
Shining like rain in the street.
In the opposite corner, young lovers meet,
Clasp hands and smile, and hymns of rapture rise.
Songs of customary peace flow from skies
That open when the hands of friendship knock.

Legions have walked here, road workers, lawyers,
Nervous fathers, apprehensive mothers,
Called from narrow apartments and green, rich gardens.
Nature summons us all to equivalence
In the democracy of birth.
New life nestles in bleached, white swaddling cloth.
The future moves through silver frames. Men grieve,
Gather books and bitter tears and leave.
Happiness melts into laneways and pain quickens.

May you, my child, live among the travellers
Who safely pass the cold reefs and the scorners
Waiting on the shores. And may your eyes always
Open with clear wonder on picturesque days
Dawning in fresh light and song.
And may you have the strength to encounter wrong,
Recognise truth and nurse the orchards of art,
And give kindness. These shattering images start
And quarrel in my soul when dear history plays.

Graduation Day

After the ceremony she moves confidently
Among her teachers, fellow students, friends,
Sisters, a brother, parents. The great tree
Shelters the courtyard. Its boughs are living hands,
Burdened with age and greenery, givers of space
And shade that lengthens into evening's calm.
Food and drinks cover tables in the classroom.
Companionable achievement lights her face.

It wasn't always so. Released from prison,
She confronted whiteboards and lecture notes with fear,
Shuffled quietly, seeming to ask strangers' pardon
For the temerity of being. Let no one draw near
And try to meet her eyes. Her family would scorn,
You'll never do it. Come back, try some ice,
Some pot. She lived expulsion from Paradise
Before she could remember, before she was born.

Her life was a succession of violent partners,
Bitter hours when love became a mockery,
The dread of separation from her daughters,
Days poisoned with alcohol, ecstasy,
Weed. In the midst of a lecture, even here
A drunk and furious man from her past came raging,
Pounding on the walls and bellowing,
Screaming in hate at what he would not share.

You showed her hope and confidence to live.
Wrestling the blindness of governments that care
Little for those who struggle most, you give
An unpretentious place where teachers dare
Restore the lonely from the rough, impoverished
Cords that choke them. Rich with fruit and green,
Your tree grows through shadows few have seen,
And nourishes her with pride at something finished.

The Bookshop

The antiquarian bookshop welcomes her
With the leisurely music of a silent room,
Shelves of literary criticism, poetry,
Old novels, art's histories, violence, peace,
Intricate design, harmony conformable
To the turbulent wind-blown orchards of the soul
Growing through rain and hail of abandonment,
Disciplined imagination that invites her eye
To follow lines' boundaries, learn their force.

She who wouldn't read and had to gather
Courage to sit and think, and dreaded
Sleep, because of the dreams,
Vivid, chimerical dreams, faces of murder,
Sudden shock of waking
To horror in terrible clarity,
And the red numbers in the clock's black depths
Blazing three.

                                    Between classes,
After classes end, she strolls the grey,
Unpretending, comfortable pavement, passes
The corner coffee shop, the surf shop, finds
Familiar harbour among avenues of learning,
Pages of strenuous thought from living minds,
Forgotten hands and bodies, pages turning,
Art unfolding shades of crucifixion,
Nativity and war, awakening day.

The Youth Worker and the Machete

1 First meeting

When they met he cursed her.

                        The timeless
Glare in the retail complex showed the perfected,
Many-coloured sterility of news and fashion.
Human lives mirrored their maker's image
In shoe store, cinema, supermarket.

He said she'd never understand
What his life was like. She couldn't help him.
No one could.

Behind his furious words walked nights
When mother was in prison, a procession of uncles.
One raped him. Drunkards punched him and roared.

Famine and the shame of illiteracy
Scarred the Centrelink office where they handed him a form.
He muttered, excused himself, ran outside, not meeting
Fellow customers' eyes. The road and the buses'
Groans sheltered him from guilt.

2 The mystery of the word

                            After twelve years'
Compulsory schooling – what happens
In classrooms and sleepy hallways,
Pale castles washed by cloudbursts and the sun,
Where teachers wander in enlightenment's bureaucracy?

After twelve years' schooling,
The political pieties of the dead,
He can't read a newspaper, the numbers that direct
A bus through its destined journey
Along loud roads or zigzagging past houses,
A timetable, a menu at Hungry Jack's.

In the twenty-first century of grace,
Words scrolling on a screen are meaningless,
Symbols of strangeness, symbols of dread.

He gropes alone through nights and days,
Heir to the word of truth,
Reason that steers the universe, the seas,
Promise of redemption from the snow,
Light from heaven that burns
In every child who endures
Or falls too soon to earth.

Illiterate exemplar of good news,
Heir to the grace to understand and know
And love, and free to choose.

3 Surprise attack

                    Everyone makes mistakes.
With a troublesome friend, in the back of a borrowed car,
Another friend driving, tearing the engine,
Slashing the wheel, signing quiet roads
With black, screeching rubber, they swerved to a stop
Beside a slim young man they thought, wrongly,
A soldier of an enemy gang. Alone with his headphones
After a day's study. He ran but they ran
Faster under the trees. Their machetes cut him,
Carved him, marked him forever despite his pleas.
They left him bleeding, broken under the trees.

                    Next day in the park,
At a table in the sun, he wept tears of remorse
For a case of mistaken identity.

4 The cinema

                    The second time,
He cursed at her again. The third morning,
Under cold lights outside the cinema,
He shrugged, sat down and they talked.

5 The verdict

The first time she visited the flat
He shared with two companions, on a concrete walkway
Lined with grey doors, austere like a prison block
High above the soil, her stomach leaped
At the maggots squirming whitely on the frayed carpet.
Pizza boxes, crusts of pizza, bongs,
Coke cans.
'Well,' she said,
'We'd better start somewhere.'

Now there are no more robberies to draw
Precarious nourishment from the shadows, no more fights.
He has given the machete away.
And when he swears,
And she reproaches him, he grins and apologises.

And now, in the twenty-first century of grace,
Child of the spirit and the streets, child of rain,
Promise of eternity, embodiment of the word,
History's answer, child of bewilderment,

He attends adult classes in a narrow building
Off a loud arterial road where traffic pulses
And growls like a predator parted from her offspring
In the fierce madness of a green rainforest's torment
Where insects howl and roasting light dances,

And learns to read.

II

Dancing with children's names

The Robbers

1

Four weeks out of work, he finds his doorstep,
Arranges backpack, plastic sheet and hat.
Falls into awkward rest.

Cars are shining enigmas, left, abandoned.
Windscreens cool and frost gathers like anger.
Thin space blankets trees.

Shifting and turning on the hardness of the hours,
He doesn't see the young men moving through alleys,
Creeping around the lights.

Young men come like shifting winter clouds,
Track closed offices. Gentle hands explore
Around a sleeping head.

2

Can the lonely and desperate, lost souls
Of midnight, steal from one more lost? He wakes.
The new sky, without thought,

Conscience or remorse, summons the skyline.
Pale buildings cut into fresh vacancy.
Light darkens the road.

Dew on the white stucco, fog on the road,
Shifting pennants of cold breath from strangers
Housed in warm coats.

Gloves, yes; thick, moist gloves. But his stolen backpack,
Pilfered hat are a brutal, raw barrenness
Slashing the bright morning.

3

She couldn't help with money, having little.
A courteous woman on her way to volunteer
To teach the young unlettered

To learn and find accomplishment and work
Under a painting of sky made by prisoners,
Dazzling with freedom and foliage,

Gave a moment's friendship and her woollen hat,
Coffee from the early morning café,
Words of commiseration,

An ear for the discontent of his troubled thought.
Tonight he returns her comfort,
Offering his groundsheet

When two young women, alone and shivering,
Meet him in the black and freezing park.
He won't ask their story,

Surrendering his last defence
Against the cold that maims, since they are menaced
By trivial, implacable frost.

Five Witnesses

1 The worker from the women's refuge

She was walking home from school (so she told me
In a garden of carob, hibiscus, camellia, grapevines)
On a country road lavish with orchards and seas
Of mauve blossom in a shallow valley
Under low hills. Cloud directed its shadow
Gently across the land. Dusty cars
And dusty trucks passed her, their music thudding.
A quiet afternoon; but you never knew
What you would find at home. So she told me,
Sitting in the garden at the refuge,
Children's voices piping from the crèche,
Carob gathering green leaves from the sun,
And spring touching city towers with ice.

I don't like to remember. When she returned,
She found her toys, her pets, her bedroom burned,
Her brother dying in his blood. Her parents
Vanished. So she told me, in the refuge from violence.
I took a golden wreath from a green oak,
Placed it around her neck. The petals spoke
Mysteries of grief, unfathomable play,
Children's voices quarrelling in the changing day.

2 The fellow user

I met her in the April drizzle
In the karri forest. Steep trees
Were grey above us. Deep, pale
Boughs, networks of orchids,
Cold ferns and sudden, brilliant
Flowers and a hidden bird's
Fluting. She was in withdrawal,
Hard recovery, wanting
The needle's sting, and mourned
For others, and she was nervous.
There in the forest, cool, patient
Of the seasons' growth, we remembered
Friends, loved friends who had fallen

To overdose or murder. Sleep
Came on them and they died.
Scarred by fire, too trusting
Of the savage tides' promise,
Let them lie abandoned under secret
Earth, or their ashes drift
Into river, garden, sea.

Waves washed aged, brown rocks
With freshness, salt and light.
Foam hurtled through clefts
Buffeting sand and seaweed
And under raw arches.
Water streamed into caves.
We stood on the white shore,
Remembered the blind currents
That engulfed our friends. Golden
Stones nestled among white flowers.

3 The classmate

A mural in the training room showed our ancestors
Dying at Gallipoli,
Blood, khaki, many wounded, and stretcher bearers
Labouring desperately

Under fire for the maimed and bleeding. The sun burned
Rough ripples, a trampled beach.
When the trainer had ended and we'd learned
All that he had to teach,

We talked at the long table while the class emptied.
A woman had soothed her heart,
Seemed for a moment to quench the ancient need
That branded her as apart

From all but the broken. In a bedroom with cold
Wooden floors and thin
Blankets she lived the slow music of old –
Profound, electric skin,

Songs of fire. They woke together, but when
Night fell, she had left.
White stars promised she wouldn't come again,
Sister of stone, bereft

Of tenderness. Soldiers shouted with no sound.
Outside the training centre
Tangled roses grew in a narrow ground,
Ripening through winter.

4 The community service manager

I frowned at my managerial desk. That morning
She hadn't been there to welcome me
With the fresh light, waving from the wall
When I steered into the driveway. At noon
Two police officers came
With word of her death. The painted
Walls accused me. Whom
Must we notify, whom should we blame?
The knife lay beside her, an empty
Syringe on the floor.
One October
Evening she brought me a white rose,
Set it on my desk in a golden vase,
A memory of the sea. I taught her to paint.
She decked the hostel walls with deep
Whirlpools, ferns and orchids, faint
Spray over rocks, a child, a child asleep.

5 The psychologist

After the memorial service in a small chapel,
I paced beside the river. White yachts flew
From sunlight into silence. The wind's tranquil
Rippling ruffled buildings where murder grew
At polished tables, and death chaired the meetings.
My thought gestured, sailed, settled, and under
Numb fire came the kindness of angels' wings
That bent with graceful songs to comfort her
And praise her. Mother of God tended her sores
With oil and white petals, caresses of light.
The sacred tree flowered. The Cross endures
History, angry strangers, the lost bird's flight.

The Hospital

She woke me from the ignorance of sleep,
Blankness, nothingness, unremembered dreams,
Night's chaos, with a rattling on my door
At three. I yawned and opened. There she stood,
Fourteen, Aboriginal, nervous, pregnant.
Streetlights formed cloudy circles on the grass
And empty pavements. Could I help her? Why
Not, pale bushes answered. Please come in.

She was hungry. I made tea and sandwiches.
The burning, shadowy towers of the hospital
Lowered over the black park, the lakes,
Remote planets and helpless stars. Troubled,
She'd called there. Triage nurses had turned her away
With sneering condescension in the hours of earth.
Where might she go? Would she be safe? These puzzles
Hadn't touched their thoughts. Unreachable stars
Glimmer in the night, and predators stalk
The hours like terrorists brooding on crazy wrongs,
Sleep and dream behind doors whitened by moonlight.

Had she a home? No home. A relative?
A friend? She remembered an aunt in a distant suburb,
Maternal and hospitable. She is kind.
She'll understand what's happening. So we drove
From western darkness into eastern night,
Beside lightless rivers, over a naked, grey,
Unpeopled bridge and past sleeping houses,
Car yards and motels, bare streets alive
With mystery, enigmas of the dawn.
Often things, she assured me, turn out best.
She'd chosen mine from a nightmare of riddling doors
And I had helped her. Then we reached her aunt,
The first half light growing from behind cold hills.

Parked beside the river, I saw the sunrise
Flooding the unhappy town with gentle fire,
Waking apartment blocks to throw long shadows,
Revealing leafy roads. Dark water lapped
Around low, restless walls. Fragments of gold
Struck jetties, rusty buoys and sullen moorings.

The Rope

Not yet twenty but old, his hollow eyes
Creased in caverns of gaunt, faded skin,
Hung in a white T-shirt and loose jeans,
Thin arms trembling, he waits on the pavement
Outside the rehabilitation centre.

Weed and wine and mixer drinks at twelve,
Three years of methamphetamine and fights,
Climaxes of anger, futile injuries,
Meaningless hours in classrooms, quadratic equations,
Circles and tangents passing over thoughts
Numbed or deafened by anguish make his life.

Windows looming over roads that curl around hills
And enigmatic houses towards the beach,
Unearthly sand, sun caressing strange mornings,
And sexual abuse by mother's friend,
Who, popular in football club and church,
Successful at insurance, guards himself
Against his guilt with bonhomie and threats,
A straggling beard and kindness to troubled children.

                                    The young man strolls
Around the cul-de-sac where drivers looking
For parks circle and mutter. He hesitates
At the open door, the foyer, the walled courtyard.

                            Like the mountaineer
He dreamed of when the cloudy hours of sleep
Opened on a fractured, ruthless dawn,
The first cars revving and birds gossiping
In quiet trees untouched by grief or rage,
Indecision or memory, hunger or pain,
Disgust or sexual shame, green branches of joy,
The climber facing a steep, plunging chasm
On a sloping edge where stones slip and roll
And tangled bushes lean over emptiness,
Facing a tenuous rope that sways across
The shattering abyss to a granite path
Winding into the light of a white-capped peak,
He knows he has three dreadful tasks.

                    The first
To grasp the fraying cord and step out
Into the cold fire.

                        The second, placing
One hand over the next, to continue the slow,
Precarious climb upward over terror.
Then to find courage to grasp the unknown arms
That reach forward at last to help him to safety.

Alps and unseen Everests of time to come
Tower in the sleeping skies. He walks through the gate.

Reunion

We come back to the school. And now the buildings,
Paths, pillars, mosaics that catch the sudden
Sun's clarity seem smaller. Half-forgotten,
Half-remembered histories and settings
Of learning and conflict rise to life and flower,
Circle, diamond, line, serpent and square
Dancing with children's names and fierce colour.
I find my name in childish letters where

I painted it and others sketched our lives,
Memorials of our histories, marks of our worlds
On pillars and plaques in whites, greens and golds,
Absorbed in youthful craft. And the changeable leaves
We and those before us planted and watered,
Brightness for the sand around a grey hall,
Stretch and beckon greenly. Innocence slaughtered,
Footballs and basketballs bounced across the oval.

Generations of the young, refugees
From uncivil war and desert camp and hunger,
Found shelter in the country of the stranger,
Iraqi, Serb, Croatian, Sudanese,
And refugees from the ruin of the West's
Ardently, truthfully achieved pages
Who drew in deprivation at their mothers' breasts.
The assembly hall is framed with images

Of past explorations, and groups of laughing students.
No one could know this boy has been abused
By a broken cousin, that girl had grown used
To fear, or tell these children have seen their parents
Savaged by holy Sudanese militias.
Observe the faces, listen and watch and see.
And here are cheerful pupils, constant teachers,
Fathers and mothers watching anxiously.

Remember our peers. In other suburbs, children
Choke in clouds of night, learn rage and hate,
Drugs and the deadly trivia of the internet,
Burglary, murder. Many come to prison,
Suicide and agony. Mental illness
Mounts in neat, implacable numbers
Through tables and annual reports. Our happiness
Endures, where children's emblems decorate pillars.

The Answer

A teacher sits and kneads and knits her high,
Evanescent, youthful hair and questions
The notice boards and tables in the staff room, 'Why
Does that child not finish her homework? Why?'
Under the infinite gaze of a thousand heavens
Twinkling and receding with emeralds and psalms,
Groves of galaxies, amaranths and palms
And the stillness of God, she breathes her infinite sigh
To the mundane morning. And another teacher answers,

'Because she hasn't eaten, because she hungers,
Because her father was evicted and they sleep near the beach
In a parked van under incommunicable mists,
Hearing the cold, unruly surf breaking,
Roaring to its slow and sudden soft falling
There below the grass and cars' exhausts
That burn the quiet and blackness, what we teach
Must battle like seedlings in a wilderness of thorn
Left by negligent gardeners to taunt unborn
Generations of leaves. Let ours be the patience
That feeds and gathers learning out of torments.'

Seven Silent Women

Why won't they speak to me? Why must they turn
Unfeeling backs against me? On the grassed square
Outside the prison library, a magpie teaches
Its child the timeless ways of the feathered inheritance
With squawks, maternal pecks and flutterings.

                            Black and white
Wings, a jabbing beak and cold, sharp eyes
Brighten morning with certainties that nature
Carries from forgotten ages into the aching
Immediacy of this, the sun, the hours,
The seven women who stand facing the barbed
Wire fence, their backs turned on me,

On me, the child-killer, shunned, rejected by the living,
Bruised women who ache for their children,
Torn from their children in the savage name of justice,
Mothers no more, mothers always, forever,
Hundreds of raw, hot miles from their children,
In the squalid rituals of custody.

                            And through the window,
Books sleep on the shelves and tables dream.
Prisoners' paintings flower on pale walls.
A sculpted dolphin in polished wood of olive
Frolics, caught in a moment that passed
And ended years ago, that never happened
And lives in the stillness of love and imagination.

I've heard them talking,
Though they won't let me join them, in the morning,
In the evening over meals and mugs of coffee,
In the spurious intimacy of a crowded cell.
Here in the women's prison,
Children fill mothers' memories. Some have lost
Sons and daughters to men choked by violence,
Some to the desperate caring of the state,
Some to the bitter void of a thousand miles.

All must wait
In anguished hope to find them again,
Strangers, so it may be, after years
Or awkward months. And some have visits,
Intermittently, under supervision,
Dull, intrusive searches for drugs and weapons.
Others wait and wonder.

My children were the brightest
Ardour of the sun,
Delicacy of stone,
Light trembling in the valleys
On a sudden morning of earth's green music.

Why won't they speak to me? Seven women
Line the horizon, their backs turned against me.
The days I lived with my children
Seem another vision, an unknown country
Lost under waves five thousand years ago,
Or overwhelmed by merciless yellow sands
That bury innocent days in hot confusion.

The days I lived with my children
Are ruthless and vivid as trees illumined by lightning
That breaks through the sky in a black rainstorm.
Trees wave and dance in the fire from heaven.

The magpie scolds its child. The dolphin springs.
The fence burns in the summer of captivity.
Seven silent women line the horizon.
Why won't they speak to me?

In a Mist

At the head of a shining table he lifts his glass
Of clear water, since he dares not sip
Alcohol, fearing that he may slip
And crumble back to sleeping on the wet grass
Where he fell, or on park benches. Silent calls
For us to stay and listen haunt his gaze.
His loved, incongruous jazz plays melodies
From New Orleans, Chicago. Trumpets blaze,
Bass patters. And invisible histories
Of murder and betrayal veil the walls.

Bodies killed in a merciless gang war
Lie on Melbourne pavements or in cafés.
Lost souls of the underworld drift through days
Patrolling strip club, massage parlour, sex store.
He ruled the night with torture and white powder.
A man he'd maimed arrived to testify
Against him, looked across the courtroom's well
Of empty light towards him, met his eye
And could not speak. But soon or late a cell
Must lock its doors on the wisest, cruellest killer.

Our conversation settles on Louis Armstrong,
Bix Beiderbecke, the legends of old Storyville.
A young girl dances naked in a brothel
While Jelly Roll Morton plays a delicate song,
Absorbed in beauty. Jail held him for decades.
And then the bottle's worse imprisonment,
Petty burglaries breaking families' peace,
Till rehabilitation hostel, treatment
Brought him the addict's tenuous release,
Conditional discharge from the clutching shades.

The lamp echoes from wooden, polished corners.
A social worker in a shelter for the homeless,
In the secrecy of the clenched heart he teaches
Abused and scarred young men to rob from strangers
And carry him their spoils, enforcing silence
With eyes that speak of years of agony.
But all around his fog of blackness, light
Pours from his colleagues who work endlessly
To counsel and give life. We say goodnight.
The trumpets fade. He falls into his darkness.

The Horses of Achilles

The squat is her last refuge. Long abandoned,
It crumbles and dissolves towards its death
Slowly and sadly, breathing quiet air
Through broken windows, the veranda's red concrete,
Greying wooden posts and cobwebbed lintels
Unobtrusively sighing. In the corner where she sleeps,
The dying walls are brightened with her choice of posters
Above her quilted sleeping bag, her clothes
Neatly folded. The mantelpiece cracks
Under the burden of invisible picture frames,
Lost treasures of the conquered.

                        Textbooks and study notes
Lie on the floor around her. At a table salvaged
From a sandy verge, she works towards the future she clutches
With grim young hands, the future that rushes from her
As she grasps it and drags it back, laughing in scorn
Of a thousand years endured in twenty-four.

                        He will find her.
Tumescent and terribly smiling, when she was three
He found her hiding and trembling under her bedclothes
In the room that was no longer hers. Year after year,
Birthday after birthday the terror happened.
Music consoled her and sport numbed her.

And when she was seventeen and she shared a house
With friends and pets, he found her, and in a narrow
Apartment on the seventh floor, overlooking
Pale roofs, gardens, trees brushing emptiness
With clumped, dark leaves, an artificial lake,
Swans and their cygnets parading like miniature warships
On a miniature sea surrounded by continents of grass.

                              He leaves his office
Late, and finds his car
In the cavernous basement. Its blank concrete,
Barren lights beckon him to the blackness
Of the dazzling black city.

                              He mutters to his car,
Ascending the cold, winding ramp
Uncounted strangers and enemies have driven before him.
'Old companion, carry me through this night
Safely. I fear the madness of the traffic,
The deathly mystery of the bridges.'

                              And gifted this once
With speech, like Achilles' horses long ago,
When he drove them at last into battle and they promised him
Victory this time, this time, but not forever,
Pistons, cylinders, spark plugs answer him,
Bright wheels whirling through fierce night like bombers
Roaring toward destruction:

                        'Yes, this time
We shall take you to your daughter. This black evening,
Once more you shall wreak your wickedness. Yes, once more,
One more hour of stupid, sordid cruelty. Tears and horror
Will fail again to move you. Not forever.
Soon there will be an emptiness where your daughter
Lived and breathed and shuddered. You have shadowed her
From home to house to apartment, to desperate squat
Where rain drips through cracked and missing tiles
And the carpet shrivels and moulders like history.
Soon she will die. You will speak
Lies at her funeral, dressed in your finest suit,
Murderous face flushed with the semblance of grief,
In a prayerful chapel under sympathetic lights.
Some will admire your courage.'

                        With no more words,
Engine and wheels continue his remorseless road.

Persephone at Admissions

Frightened, anxious and young,
                          so violently young,

She hobbles to the green entrance of the maternity hospital
Through clouds of smoke, past clutches of novice mothers,
Potty-mouthed visitors swaying, swearing, laughing,

Rich tremulous life of the flowering leaves.

She carries the burden of unborn mornings and evenings,
Rented movies, takeaways and nightmares.
She gasps at the dark and yellow-lit reception desk.

'My waters broke. I think that's what it's called.
I think I'm having my baby.'

Touched by a flash of sunlight
From eternal, merciful meadows,
Looking at her uncertain friends
Hovering behind her
Like tall, young herons,

For an instant she's the image of Persephone,
Transcendent flower-goddess of too few summers,
Divinity of spring's new air, exploring
Earth's purposes and explicable mysteries
In trees, late blossoms and early, unripe fruits,
Strawberries forming under leaves,

                      That moment
She found herself in the mindless grip of the underworld's
Vengeful, reluctant king,

Torn from pleasant fields of rose and parsley,
Branching vines and daisies that open
As if there were no other seasons,
Lilies and violets she scattered into baskets
With her friends, or cherished like childish treasures
In the green folds of her dress,
Whirled by arms of thoughtless strong passion
That stared and grinned without reason,

                        Dreading
The journey in the deadly chariot
Past pools of sulphur and salt lakes,
Past the misty river and the three heads
Of Cerberus howling.

                                    One mouth offers drugs'
Tenuous vigour, spurious visions, bliss
That wakes to a dry-mouthed haze. The second,
Endless gulfs of self-laceration,
Black gales of self-reproach. The third dog's jaw
Bays and barks of hot, unresting need
Never to be filled, never caring.

                                      Once fertile fields,
Famed for their loveliness, loved for their legendary harvests
Of grain and peace and music,
Seeds of genuine rapture,
Lie shrivelled and dying among thistles and harsh grasses.

The madness of the old gods condemned them,
Consigned her to screaming mornings,
Nappies and sleepless midnights,
Days and evenings of hunger,
Addictions, withdrawals, violence and fear.

                        A long story,
Hymned by a child of Homer,
Written by Ovid, poet of adultery and exile,
And carved on an Italian wall.
A sculpted tear, a backward glance,
Not quite imperishable tribute to the passing flowers,
Laboured in marble four hundred years ago.

Uncertainly, guided by experienced, friendly arms,
Mother who has never come here before,
Child who has had no classes, brought no belongings,
Bewildered innocence in a stained T-shirt,

Passes from view in the slow, shuddering lift.

III

Sketches from the front line

Sketches from the front line

1 Charlene

Day is drawing towards a cool September evening. Charlene is walking with her three small children towards McDonald's. Her three children have – this is not uncommon – three different fathers. Or, to be more precise, they don't have three different fathers.

Two are seldom or never seen or heard from. One pays irregular unreliable amounts of child support and is otherwise never heard from. All this involves Charlene in lengthy, frequent disagreements with Centrelink, in dispirited queuing in a wide, impersonal, low ceilinged waiting area with an artificial palm in a wooden basket. And in the sadly irregular arrival of income.

She and her children move intermittently from one shared rental to another. Sometimes her numerous fines – the products of traffic offences, drug dealing on a very small scale, an occasional fight and other peccadilloes – follow her from one address to another, sometimes not. So she is often behind in paying them, or unaware of them.

The road grows gradually chillier in the lengthening afternoon. Honeyeaters jump and browse among the bottlebrushes. Dark rose leaves flow in soporific gardens. Three children and their mother walk peacefully – with as much peace as they have ever known – on the fading concrete pavement.

A police car slides towards them and stops. Two young officers emerge and approach Charlene, who, as we know, has unpaid fines on her record, and, in part, on her conscience.

They lead her into the car and drive away. Three small children find themselves suddenly bereft on the roadside, alone, frightened, crying.

2 Robert

He wakes slowly, imperceptibly, as dawn's silvery greyness begins to threaten the juvenile detention centre's undistinguished buildings with day. His customary place of residence is thousands of kilometres away in a community surrounded by red earth, harsh pale grasses and immemorial hills, where he lives with his father.

Aged fifteen, he has been abused by an uncle since his infancy. For many years he has dulled consciousness and anguish by sniffing petrol. His thoughts and his words form slowly, like gradual black shadows rising between sunlit clouds, broken by bright, fiery currents of anger and desire.

He forms the thought slowly, formulates it carefully, that here in the detention centre, for the first time he can remember, he feels safe.

3 Zachary

How many government departments are there? In his thirteen years of life Zachary has encountered more than two dozen of them. Agency after agency, social worker after social worker, teacher after teacher, discovering his drug-addicted father, his sex worker mother, his older brother the gang member, their broad, unfocused, collective familial rage and Zachary's own violent, incomprehensible temper, have resolved that it is all too difficult and turned away. They have, after all, their procedures, and they are judged, and they placate their self-esteem, by results.

Well for Zachary that he is already, not yet fourteen, a habitué of the children's court that glows in the dull sun near the sprawling, sleeping railway tracks. It is while awaiting one of his courtroom appearances that he makes the acquaintance of a police constable from the local police and community youth centre.

Constant, humane, understanding, she achieves a friendship. She carefully nurtures his confidence, giving time and courtesy where others have followed their training. In three months he will be absorbed in acquiring skills in electronics. In five months his parents will greet her as a welcome, kindly guest.

4 Louella

Below the lumbering faux marble statuary of the department store a child reaches tremulous fingers for an imaginary parent's absent hand. Hoarse, stumbling, rough voices bellow their meaningless, hopeless quarrels across the shadowy mall. Shoe shops, boardwalks, lingerie shops, movie posters. Thoughtless, remorseless lunch hour in the CBD.

5 Helen

Forty thousand years ago a fire, guarded by piled stones, hissed and crackled into warmth not far from this spot. Surrounded by supermarkets, soaring banal cinemas, vacant, dispirited shoppers and eager shoppers, Helen sits at a table in a coffee shop with the lady from the training service. Helen, nineteen, answers questions about her past and her schooling uncertainly, with uneasy pauses and with moments when her voice falls to inaudibility.

Asked what she wants to do, she is clear and she suddenly looks forward, her vision lightened by thoughts of what in the last three years, amidst shock, bereavement and the glaring lights' darkness, has given her strength. 'I want to learn to help others,' she says. 'To help other young people, well, get their lives on course. As (here she names two unacclaimed heroes, passionate women of vigorous humanity from the modestly funded outreach service) helped me.'

IV

Soldiers of compassion

Homage to an Outreach Worker

1

Assembled in a converted old school hall,
Far from the lavish boardrooms of the Terrace,
I look around from face to friendly face,
Pioneers of courage. One and all,
Or all but one, experienced in the spreading,
Hidden struggle, unromantic, long,
With cruel weather that traps too many young
In rains of cultural collapse, their wise words, shedding
Warmth and light on brutal suffering, wake
The rational joy that those who venture make.

Cups, glasses and notepads strewn before us,
The stranger here pronounces (meaning well),
'It's too late when they're fifteen.' Voices swell
Immediately, indignantly, a chorus
Of fire, sparking around the room with rage
For empathy and reason. They have seen
Children, adults, seventeen, nineteen
Or thirty begin to recover and assuage
Neglect and molestation, walk from prison
And touch their friends with words to move and soften.

2

Consider me, then. I won't see fifteen
Or forty-five again. And still I pray
There's hope for me when I wake every day
To raw pain. And suddenly I'm called back to green
And gently sloping grass, a quiet road,
An hour's conversation. As I broker
Peace between my colleagues and our visitor,
I remember what that conversation showed,
The story of a man who offers outreach
To young addicts on town square, corner, beach.

His face bears the lines of a dozen lifetimes.
Filigreed road maps to nowhere etch gaunt cheeks.
His tone is hoarse but welcoming as he speaks,
Telling what he's seen, graves, pointless crimes.
And I, who have endured a decade, more,
Of agony broken by gales of violence,
Listen to the faithful evidence
He carries from the front lines of a war
Seldom noticed, seldom reported, storms
Of desperation, unremembered harms.

After twenty years of using, clean
For half that time since then, he tours the streets,
Gives gentle words to teenagers he meets
Travelling the terrible paths to death between
Hunger and cloudy dreaming, paths he's known
And marked with blood and rain. Traces
Of love show the courage he embraces
And mirrors to the stolen and the wind-blown.
A child grey from heroin appals
His memory and the thin years he recalls.

3

This year the trees are flowering early. Winter
Will come upon us soon, high branches thrash,
The rivers rise and power lines break and crash.
These tables and this meeting are the centre
Of all that is and is to come. We rise
And go to where fresh sandwiches await.
Around the nation harrowing winds and fate
Contend before uncomprehending eyes.
How costly my fortune, knowing such women
And men, war-torn soldiers of compassion.

Homage to a Midwife

How did my baby, crumpled, breathing, strong,
Ignorant of his defencelessness, his need,
Soft as the songs of earth, mottled baby that I
Could hold in my hand, survive?

                       I was sixteen.
I slept in a public toilet and washed in the basins,
Rinsed my laundry under cold water in the basins,
Slept on the frigid tiles in the night air
And chemical smells, until council workers found me.
Then they came each twilight and locked the doors.
Heroin sold me meretricious bliss.
Meretricious, I traded my flesh for food and dreams.

                     Alone on the street,
In cars and shelters, in cafés and in parks,
Cinemas flashing and shouting with morality,
Alone and fractured, I said to myself that I
Might bear a child and fill my life with love,
That I would love my child, my child love me.
Love would illuminate the anger of the sun.

Surprised to find I share your history,
Where you might have expected only a brisk,
Impersonal doctor smiling across the desk,
Teenage, pregnant, unnerved, you talk to me.

Alone and frightened, novice as you are now,
I dreamed uneasy dreams beside the river,
Fled from parent, teacher, sister, brother;
Dazed, watched the circling torn leaves rise and flow.

All this, for me, was thirteen years ago.
I carry the stigmata of distress,
The scars of other years' unhappiness.
Still I resolved to fight and learn and know.

Look outside my surgery window – there,
Four swans lifting in formation,
Living arrows of accurate flight and passion,
Wings persuading unforeseeable air.

                                  When they found I was pregnant,
They let me stay at the refuge, the kind women
Juggling beds and escapees from the rain,
Bureaucrats' suspicions and official forms.

Grey feathers scuffle,
Flower in the flowing tree-tops
Like promises of distant fields,
Or grace-notes to the chants of mid-day.

They introduced me to a midwife whose depths and wisdom
Taught me feeding, nappies and all the rest,
Creams and powders. She inveigled me
Back to lessons and then to university,
Time for nutrition and a house shared with friends.
Will they take my baby, the guardians of morning,
Protectors who betray children into foster homes,
Shift them and their grief from placement to placement,
Custodians of the helpless? That was my fearful
Question. Not if I
Got clean and stayed clean. So she promised me.

Stethoscopes, computers and thermometers,
Drug company samples, photos and records of illness,
Death and recovery surround me in the sunlight.
I receive the humbled intimacies of the old,
Stammered burdens of the young.

Expectant at seventeen, you talk to me,
Adept of the streets and bitterness,
Grieved and numb and made to feel worthless.
But only those who scorn you shame their worth.

Three months out from the waiting hour of birth,
You endure a limitless map of possibility,
Pride and courage and contingency,
Mother of mystery, child of wings and breath.

Homage to a Youth Worker

1

Furious at opposite ends
Of a table overlooking
The patient, prayerful currents'
Green, grey and drifting
Worlds of sunlit blue,
A vacant, pale beach
Marked by tracks of unanswering
White platoons of birds
And enigmatic snakes'
Thin, meandering errands,

2

Frozen in a clench of rage, fourteen-year-old
Avoids her mother's eyes while centuries
Turn, and builders construct palaces,
Demolition teams ruin them, revolutions
Slaughter their millions and wars crush
Fallen civilisations. Living souls
In their tens of millions suffer each her unique
Bereavement, agonies, death. Proscribed libraries stand
Untenanted, patient and prayerful like the currents,
Waiting for the footsteps of the faithful
When armies of positivist guards shall let drop their rifles
And re-education camps become farmland.

3

Memories savage her thought like waves buffeting wet rocks,
Unconscious, prayerful, driven by the deep currents' flow,
Lifted by wind and the witless moon. Her fourteen years,
Fourteen aeons haunt her with sudden harsh voices
In the blackness of night in a refugee camp, torn canvas,
Rough blows and rape. They haunt her with father's death,
Crunch and patter of gunfire, buckets, mud and hunger,
Weeks with little sleep, and how mother once traded
A diamond bracelet for milk. Dying wreaths of dry trees,
Vistas of the scarred and starving.

                              Then the dawning shock
Of a menacing language, new words, culture that is no
Culture, but a sunlit desert; shallow sand of drugs;
Quicksand of ignorance, noise and sex that arrived
To terrify her, so that for twelve months she stayed
In her bedroom, refused to speak.

                              And after that she immersed
Her soul in the sinking waste that burned around her, drawing her
Into drifts of cannabis, flames of ice, taunting nights of desire.

Through geological ages, while jarring images rise,
Clash, foam and settle back into mysterious currents,
She watches and turns her face and her hidden tears from mother
And the sorrow of time. Coral reefs spread under rippling
Blue wavelets. Schools of painting grow and crumble
Into academic conventions.

          Only once in ten thousand years
A javelin of the sun catches a pelican
Falling, a plummet of white
Between black clouds, black rocks and pearl-green sea.

4

Survivor, mother, fugitive
From outspread farms and market towns,
Odorous, groaning herds,
Cold stars over grey fields,
Unattainable, familiar light,
Small moon and white roads
And by day the towering, militant sun.

Survivor, mother, fugitive
Who sailed on the dry wind
From a refugee camp in the north,
Past knives of bereavement, carried
On steel wings of love,
Community and faith, she wakes
In the slow Australian night,
Shuddering for her daughter,

Who turns away through harsh,
Unreasonable generations
And will not touch her.

5

You leave your office in an abandoned school,
Take your car from the grass below drowsing trees,
Drive to meet mother
At a table above the restless, troublesome shore
Where sea-nymphs dance with sun-gold, streaming hair
On the white sand, the brown, weed-strewn rocks,
Between strollers by the tides who never glimpse them,
Dance to the morning's changeable symphony of waves.

With the warmth of years you listen to her fractured story,
Words wrenched by bereavement, articulate tears.
You embark on the slow journey through lifetimes
To the other side of the table where you find
Daughter's percussive fingers and sit beside her
As galaxies burn to constellations of ash
And the tide wells, whispering its green ephemera.
You raise her hand to place it in her mother's hand.
They meet at the far end of the infinite,
Bleached, grey table, streaked by white stains
From inconsequent, departed birds. Gulls cry regal ecstasies
To the flow of the nymphs' minuet. They embrace,
And daughter begins the voyage of a thousand autumns
And doubtful winters, to school, home and tomorrow.

The Anniversary

When she had suffered in and out of prison
Ten of her twenty-eight years, and never free
More than occasional precarious, frightened months,

Angry, precarious months; and before those days
Juvenile detention, childhood terror – but why
Harry her back to the violated privacies

Of hunger, fear, abuse, infant dismay?
They set her free when the bird of paradise flowered,
Its dark and gold pointed blossoms laughing

On their long stems in peaceful garden beds
Under the quiet walls of a former convent.
Meeting her there, you and your two colleagues

Guided her past eruptions and precipices of rage,
Separation from heroin's solitary warmth,
Through labyrinths of memory and distress.

Today the bird of paradise flowers again
In the convent garden and brilliant butterflies whirl
Their temporary dance around the passing leaves,

Black, white and golden wings unfolding.
Hydrangeas call borrowed light to their blue shells,
And she touches your arm and marks one year of freedom.

V

Hymning the sun

The Grieving Stone

Uncanny magic shaped this stone,
A wet rock in a stream brushed by grey
And silver branches through hot light of day
        And morning's moan.
Dragonflies hunt around it, insects thieve,
Marsupials tremble in small bushes' rays.
Bright lizards drowse where passing sunlight plays.
Whoever touches the stone shall never grieve.

And hour by hour, you'll stroll where leaf
And petal shelter drug dealers and children,
Paint sniffers bow their heads in a green garden,
        And not know grief.
Stray cats quarrel in a laneway. Disease
Pounces, minds crumble. Tragedy falls
On couch and doorway, bleak graffitied walls;
Earth where a drunk sleeps under pine trees;

Courthouse steps. Under the high
Passion of the sun you'll watch light's order,
A van, three guards, a sweat-stained prisoner,
        Without a sigh.
The law shudders. Lies will harrow the land,
Families mourn and generations flee,
And you'll look calmly, smile impassively,
Ruined by the stone, the wasteful sand.

The Power to Lie

Burdened by Providence with the power to lie,
He spoke in boardrooms and meeting rooms, acquired
Many things and nothing, laboured and grew tired.
Asleep one night he dreamed his mind could fly.
His memories left the soil. He greeted the sky,
Welcomed the clouds like a lover always desired
And never touched. He woke alone, inspired
To change his faith. Given the grace to die,

He saw the thousands he'd lied to gathered on a low
Hilltop, their backs towards him, hymning the sun.
They turned, and each wore his own troubled eyes,
More loneliness and bereavement than he could know.
Their histories rose like a choir on the horizon,
Ungathered songs and squandered harmonies.

The Evaluator

This is the building. You from the department of earth,
You from the department of sand, come in with me.
I put aside my wings of order and faith,
Flesh of hours the sun mirrors playfully
With the weaving flames of its corona and its core,
Robes made from words and satin to describe a path
To rational ecstasies of heaven, and the songs I wore
In gardens and to court the stars. Now, dressed
In a dark suit, open-necked shirt, as a young
Consultant I approach to evaluate and test.
A room awake with the passionate unsung

Opens its windows on a stony, leaf-strewn courtyard.
Two officers from two departments of state
Accompany me. And we sit at a levelling, hard,
Functional table. Uncertain faces wait.
I begin my questions. You that work with the lost,
The desperate, can you capture in a word,
A phrase, a narrative, what you cherish most
Of what you've known, accomplished, the death you conquer?
And someone speaks to me. 'When night arrives,
Cooling the hot street, and children wander
Without home, comfort or nourishment, we save lives.

'When humid air surrounds slow traffic and weighs
Warmly on the young who have endured
More than young years should by nights and days,
We labour. Here's a story. Bruised and scored
By knife wounds, a teenage boy limps up and asks
For ointments, stitches, bandages. He displays
Blaring symptoms of battle and neglect. He risks
Talking to us, shyly, while we mend
Torn skin. He sells his flesh to unhappy human
Predators, unprotected. We attend
Calmly, teach him safety.' So the woman

From the mobile medical service smiles and murmurs
With all the kind intensity of truth.
The boy came back. They led him to new ventures
In learning, shelter from the stern rain, human worth.
The timeless years, the motionless dance of light,
Heaven's undying grief and mercy's flowers
Grow around her voice in the pale room's quiet.
Is there another who can witness? One, young and grey,
Describes his outreach to the young and grim,
Prematurely cold drug addicts, how he'll say
Consoling words, teach health, save pulse and limb.

His was the shock of memory and lost souls.
You from the department of sand, you drowse, you sigh.
I watch a sunlit banner as it rolls
From east to west, from south to north, a sky
Of singing silver. A young woman speaks.
'My friend and I save lives with long patrols
Through painful days and nights, unsettling weeks,
In shopping centres, refuges and shelters,
Loving homes and loveless homes, in nurseries
And hospitals. We work with teenage mothers,
Younger than teenage mothers, and their babies.

'Some, if not for us, would die. Neglect,
Abuse would kill them. So research has shown,
And funerals and mourning. We protect
Babies from death, their mothers from guilt, alone
And maimed by failure.' Silent melodies pour
Invisible harmonies. 'We help them to self-respect,
Bring children's babies life. Imagine the raw
Keening. Perceive you killed or lost your child
At thirteen, fourteen, fifteen. Instead you know
Your motherhood, your infant reconciled.
Maybe you're back in class. And see life grow.'

Whom shall I evaluate? You from the departments
Of earth and sand, your tired, unholy thought
Drifts like smoke away from teenage parents,
Like thin smoke passing above fences wrought
Out of iron and pragmatism and care for your careers,
Away from drug users, street kids and the countenance
Of heaven arrayed in chronicles and tears
For lives destroyed and what must be. A cloud,
Sacred and pure, of truths and witnesses
Surrounds you. Paintings of mercy sing aloud.
You lift your hearts to lies and forgetfulness.

The Music of the Streets

The closing movement of a pristine symphony soared
Through intricate sheets of mathematical flame
To a stillness where the oboe sang its name.
The solemn purity of deep strings poured
Light around the audience
And streams of melody wove towards their silence.

Appreciative friends and jealous peers surrounded
The composer in a gold, high-ceilinged foyer,
Balancing finger foods and juggling liquor.
Echoes of the truth in music sounded,
Waltzing, whirling. A thousand dancers,
Dressed in silk and fire, the song of trumpeters,

Violinists' memories, the warm
French horn, the rumble of the tympanum
Played around the walls above the hum
Of idle voices, filled my thoughts with form
And rhythm's delicate force. Rich themes
And tragedy harmonised, then brilliant gleams,

Sudden waves of piercing vision broke
And sighed. 'A timeless sadness floods my heart
When I orchestrate and give each horn its part,
Each string, percussion, reed.' The composer spoke,
His eyes alive with sombre praise,
Memories of bare, sharp, hungry days

None of us could imagine. 'Long ago,
My music was discordant screeches, groans,
Mechanical and electronic tones,
Disharmonies drawn violently from the bow
In soundscapes of mindlessness,
Jarred and breaking rhythms, howls of distress

'Portraying what I dreamed. I saw the void
Opening its terrible chasm under thought
And action. Callow despair was the sound I taught
And I mocked the growing flowers, saw unalloyed
Darkness in the dawning light.
My compositions mirrored shame and spite.

'Centuries ago the music of the spheres
Gave universal harmony to all
The stars and planets. They danced at its call,
Love guided them. But now it disappears –
My youthful wisdom said to me –
Vanished in the glare of astronomy.

'The clarity of arithmetic meant no more
Than conventions evolved to let the greedy grow.
The Milky Way a stridency of thermo-
Nuclear fusion, random blare and roar
Of huge destruction. Selfless
Love a fiction, logic foolishness,

'The universe a chaos, truth a dream,
Neutrons whirled by chance. And so my song
Was bitterness and agony and wrong,
Jagged stones hurled into a dusty stream,
Irrational numbers. Concerts died,
Friends and family left. My groundless pride

'Followed me into the homelessness of hell.
No wife, no love, no children. I slept on the road,
In alleys and in doorways, under my load
Of ignorance. When winter's blind rain fell,
I crawled under crumbling stone.
I queued for breakfast, standing proud and alone

'Among my new-found friends. Slowly I learned
To comfort others. Harder, to accept
Comfort from others whom cold seas had swept
Onto these shattering rocks, and my shame returned.
I met a young boy with nowhere,
Nothing, and I helped him to a shelter.

'I met a young woman with her baby,
Friendless in a raw, untenanted building.
She bent and crooned to the child she was feeding,
Then turned aside and muttered wordlessly.
I walked for miles to find someone
To patch what generations had undone.

'And so I learned that truth is suffering,
Love and help and healing. Every soul
Plays its theme in passion, one and whole
Though broken, breaking, houseless, wandering.
This is the irreducible harmony,
Despite the lost who will not hear or see.

'They have their music. Cardinal numbers burn
For each one on the street, each two or three,
Every child crouching in misery.
So I began to love, to count and turn,
To harmonise again and sing
The complex logic of awakening.'

His words dropped away. But the symphony
Followed me home, the teeming night's carillon,
Diapason of the stars, the composer's passion,
The homeless child's mathematical harmony,
Trombones calling to the French horn,
Gentle flutes, poised trumpets, the deep bassoon.

The Reception

In this ephemeral mansion of stone and glass,
        shining satin tables frame a room
that looks out on a soft, polished river
        and a green, empty park, and name-tags
determine who shall sit at the high table.
        Homeless beggars walk hot streets,
argue with passers-by; some camp in stairwells.
        A speaker rises and begins,
attention fades and my mind reprehensibly strays.

I think of other hierarchies. Insurmountable,
Unapproachable Homer, master of the battlefield,
Ruler of the hexameter and the shield,
Chanter of eternal, sempiternal
Sadness, roamed in search of recognition
Through cities that quarrelled over his name when he was gone.
Alive, their citizens snubbed him mercilessly,
Island, mainland, ships in the drifting sea.

Was Homer blind from birth? No one has perceived
More sharply – the last light glimpsed in a dark forest
As a boat draws out from the shore, the hornets' nest,
The terrible face of Priam as he grieved
Ten fallen sons, his enemy's sudden kindness
Confronting losses past and the ruthlessness
Of death to come. Blood raged in the river.
The gods reclined in passion and laughter forever.

Guests taking brief refuge from bureaucratic
*   works and days in meeting rooms*
that grow no corn and nourish no one's sheep
*   stand awkwardly beside chairs,*
near tables and in burning emptinesses,
*   shuffle and pretend to listen*
to words that drift invisibly into plaster and glass.

The most vigilant philosopher of all,
Who wandered from a Scots village to Cologne,
Duns Scotus, unrivalled teacher next to the throne
Of being and the word, new thinkers would call
The original dunce. And so thought parched its stream,
Diverted into a solipsistic dream
Of consciousness in a void. He saw the body's
Grace, the loving gesture's harmonies.

Crafted fire, unprecedented gold,
Art and the ageless beauty of the ageing face.
Rembrandt, I've read, knew mornings of disgrace,
Favourite paintings, drawings piled and sold
While neighbours watched and scoffed and hours grew hard.
Scrupulous detail racked in a salesman's yard.
Art finds its fickle wealth when lifetimes pass.
Undying glories blur in fashion's glass.

Meals arrive on plates that shine like midnight
 in a bitter desert of sand and stars
and wine glows in its elegantly curved decanters.
 Armies of superficiality lift
glasses to mouths that are eager and pass like flowers
 in the savage winds of summer's rage,
drink to the tears of truth and faithfulness.

I've watched these sterile guests in their offices
Form their priorities, tend their dead careers,
Connive and plot and frame pragmatic years
With anencephalic plans. The young and homeless,
Adjudged too hard to help, shiver through the night
Of remembered cruelty, needles, hunger, flight,
Survival. But the judge who meets each mind
Restores the lost and shatters the unkind.

A light glows in the deep woods far away,
Scarlet, trembling. Injured ghosts of soldiers
Groan again in tents of forgotten wars
As Homer sails alone across the grey,
Slapping water. A young man wakes painfully,
Rises slowly, agonizingly,
From a damp bench. No one can see him, none.
His story burns on the golden pages of heaven.

Mission Statement

Artist, you shall inherit a pitiless duty.
Not to enrol in fashion's remorseless wars,
Infinitesimal rumblings on the long, hot shores,
Low waves that gnaw rough rocks of sanctity,
Forgetting the foam and blue greens of the sea,
But to find the impassable line of fire that draws
Attentive sight to glimpse the holy laws
Of timeless truth, truth's individuality
In a homeless child sleeping in a barren park
Or a manger. You stammer and speak with word and sound,
Wet paint spreads with precision over canvas,
Marble chips and falls to reveal its ground
And the blind eyes of passion. You sculpt the dark
Images, the primitive street's turbulence.

The Flood

I was a baby. I woke alone, in pain,
A bowl of mull standing on my parents' table,
A pornographic movie on the screen.
I was a child, a father at fourteen.
I hot-wired cars as soon as I was able.
I was a drunk girl, sleeping on a train.

A young policeman, facing death and blood.
A mother, mourning in a prison cell.
You that built enterprise on sands of greed,
Sold love and beauty for relief of need,
Take pride. You did your devil's work so well
That thirty centuries struggle in the flood.

The Ark

I built my craft with sails of memory,
Stitched by thoughts that came to me at the graveside.
I measured it to the tides of history,
And laid its keel with boards of wounded pride.

I beckoned wolves, camels, lizards, goats,
The gull, the egret, honeyeaters, vultures,
Elephant, rhinoceros, weasels, stoats.
I collected poems, histories, sacred scriptures.

The quoll, the scampering potoroo, the numbat,
Wide-winged eagle, sudden, chattering swifts,
Tree kangaroo, the rolling, burrowing wombat,
The long-wrought sonnet, elegy that lifts.

I saw my neighbours yawning at their wide screens,
Dead imagination in the flickering light,
Addicts burning forests, golds, reds, greens,
Fathers' forgotten bones the sun bleached white.

A fifteen-year-old child turning a trick;
A condom fallen in the weeds; the shock of ages;
An old man's house demolished brick by brick;
Human sacrifices in the city; burning pages.

I heard my neighbours taunt me, brand me wrong
To work, weighed low by dread they couldn't feel;
A gangster's snarl of loss, a drunkard's song.
I called caged lyre-birds to fly free and heal.

Through courtrooms, prison yards, detention centres,
I searched for passengers, in cell-block, leaf-washed street,
In counselling rooms, or selling *The Big Issue* on corners,
Dozing under savage bridges in the liquid heat.

When the rain began I summoned my friends to board.
I soothed the lion, talked to the seagulls, fed
Mongoose, parrot; sweated while the tides poured;
Gathered mothering sheep; shared wine and bread.

I taught my doves to fly in search of shores
At the risk of drowning; to find the olive tree,
The promise of an end to heaven's wars,
Mercy across the judgement of the sea.

Men floundered, women gurgled in the stream.
Children couldn't read; I put up signs in vain.
Visions of landfall; the mourning sailor's dream.
My loaded ship cast off in deepening rain.

Mountains of thunder; lightning's burning blades
Clashed through the sky and fired gulfs of cloud.
Waves leaped to join the rain; the steep cascades
Foamed on the wharf and bollards cracked and bowed.

Around the masts white sails of memory swirled.
Ten thousand captains turned their backs from spite.
Through tides of sadness for the wrongful world,
I sailed toward the dove's returning flight.

The Rain-tree and the Fire-tree

I followed a winding gravel path down a hillside
Stony with time. Rich ferns and lavish trees
Sheltered bright flowers. There I hoped for peace
From vivid deaths and children's suicide,
Despair and official indifference that mocks.
They die and no one hears them. Trickling lines
Of clear water fell among the rocks.
Wings and butterflies glistened through green vines.

Where the sun swayed, there it seemed that bough,
Leaf, trunk and dead wood breathed and spoke.
A tiny cry of pain when a small branch broke
Sharpened the stillness of the bush, and now
Syllables formed and pulsed through the air.
Sentences and memories that fluttered
And dropped to ground, and thought lived everywhere
Around me, and the soft water chattered.

'Mine was the wood that gave the brutal crosses
Where two thieves and the Saviour found their slow,
Ungentle deaths, and mourners watched below.
Mine were the bitter arrows and the losses
On a thousand battlegrounds since wars began,
Supple bows and laboured wooden shields,
And desperate refugees and bright blood ran,
Staining white roads and smearing muddy fields.'

So it seemed I heard an old stump sing,
Scored with open fissures, dead and bare,
Though it was half a world away from where
The tramp of Roman cruelty, the hammer's ring,
Blended with shouts of agony. What spears,
What spear-throwers, hafts of granite blades,
Came from this tree's wood in unmarked years
After it creaked and fell in the moving shades?

A karri tree sighed, 'I have witnessed crimes
Beyond endurance. Child-killers came here,
Dragging their victims, marked the soil with fear
And shock, and buried savagery that climbs
To the sun like saplings. What value has my grace,
The sweep of my pale trunk, cool morning-grey
Foliage, when memories of torture claim this place
Beneath my hungry roots, and chip brown clay?'

The grass tree laboured its black growth through centuries.
Its grey and green spikes hummed in the afternoon light.
It remembered outlived storms and the sweeping flight
Of rain that darkened and smashed streams and valleys.
'To passing generations of beast and bird
I sing my philosophies of stoicism and day's
Resolve to suffer and live and call unheard,
And a fine necklace of golden orchids strays.'

A warm, rough jarrah said, 'I also saw
Those killers, all the brutishness of men
Shown in a man's and a woman's hate. But then
Young lovers came, ardent, nervous, raw,
And families with children in their mirth
Laughing in the clinging air of autumn,
Sharing all the variousness of earth,
And bushes sighed with wallaby and possum.'

'Nothing redeems the suffering that's past,'
The karri's leaves whispered. 'No resurrection saves
The frightened children cold in mineshaft graves,
Nor me, who watched their terror and who stand, caught fast
In what I dreamed was gentle soil.' A sweet
Young vine laced with flowers ventured a song
Of summer and marriage at the ripe hill's feet.
Butterfly, shrub and marri chanted along.

A fern said, 'Watch my swaying, breathing frond.
Green and fierce, it stretches up, leans down,
One, irreplaceable. In summer, brown,
Brittle, I crumble. No one sees beyond
The shifting seasons, knows what endless peace
Or eternal silence falls when rain and cloud
Are ended and the years of violence cease,
Or whether my uniqueness sings aloud.

'Shall murdered children live to laugh once more
Beyond the forests of years, the decades' rhyme,
Insects scurrying, symphonies of time?
Death marks the drifting sand with maps of war.'
A bird swooped on a fish in a narrow creek.
The fern sighed in its harbour under the shade
Of old, bending branches murmuring bleak
Consolation to the ground while their shadows played.

It seemed I saw a tree of glistening rain,
Its trunk a weave of raindrops, branch and leaf
Of tiny drops like tears of remembered grief.
Each held a point of burning blood, its stain
Brilliant, red and echoing. The jewelled tree,
Flowing with scenes of love, bereavement, slaughter,
Miniatures of transient history,
Reflected flowers' music in its water.

'Far from here, in yards and prison cells,
Behind barbed wire, towers and gloomy walls,
On the grassed fields of mental hospitals,
People bring hope to the desperate, drawn from wells
Beyond the ken of time-serving managers,'
The rain-tree sang. 'And you are blessed to find
The waking love that heals the loveless strangers,
The gentle force that frees the captive mind.'

A tree of golden fire rustled lightly.
Its leaves were cool flames fallen from cold skies,
Dancing restlessly like clouds of birds that rise.
Flame-feathered branches glowed in harmony.
The fire-tree murmured, 'God alone gives rest.'
The bush was peaceful. Leaf and trunk were still.
Wings fluttered in the fiery shadows' nest.
I took the gravel path back up the hill,

And heard the rain-tree say, 'Take up your load
Made from the forests of time that drops like stone
On the green earth, and suffer years alone.
Do what you may to heal others' road.'
Now I imagine the voices of the wood,
The bird-song and the leaves' rippling stream,
Debating while hot tides of memory flood
The quiet sandbars in the long night's dream.

VI

A tapestry of murder

A Handful of Diamonds

Only the wounded notice. But when dawn completes
The agon of night, and the first brisk commuters
Appear on suddenly fresh, expectant streets
Between parks and offices, marching to war like soldiers,
Men, women and children without homes
Rise and leave their fragile dwellings – rooms
Constructed of cardboard and newspaper, fragile shelters.

The kindly jeweller greets them when they pass
Beside his shop on the way to the soup kitchen
Under the quiet trees on the sandy grass.
They gather in his forecourt. He hands them golden
Bracelets, wreaths of diamond, emerald, silver,
Gentle words of guidance to last forever,
Coffee and friendship, ruby, pearl, obsidian.

Arsonists prowled our city and fired selected
Shops and houses. Whether they burned from hate
Of the gentleness and courtesy God protected
But could not save from murder, or the weight
Of centuries of death, no one can tell.
And when the pounding rain and hail fell
And drenched the flames, they drenched the flames too late.

Paramedics pick their way through the smouldering
Ruins of the kindly jeweller's store,
Broken walls and cabinets, twisted, dangling
Wires, and a blackened, sodden floor.
Now for the last time, gathered and furled
In cloth, his fleshly remnants leave his world
Of craft and love that ended in the dull flames' roar.

The craftsman's suffering friends return to mourn
His fallen hands, his generosity,
His kindness. A white-robed angel stands alone
In the shattered building, holds for all to see
A handful of diamonds. They give out rare,
Unearthly light. Strange music fills the air,
Intangible songs of immortality.

Graffiti Artist

Stray birds chatter in steep canyons,
Ice burns from city windows
Into damp night. And I paint dragons
Lifting jagged wings, and rainbows,
Layered, geometric colours.
Trajectories of bullets flying,
Miniature clusters of marching soldiers,
Refugees, and brick walls dying.

I paint the city's homeless young
Wandering through its streets alone.
I show the city the dragon's tongue
Rolling over its wooden throne.
I show the blood the century scatters
Into its gutters among cigarette butts,
Food scraps, needles and newspapers.
I paint dark skin and deep, red cuts.

In the green park, swirling bees
Collect new pollen out of soft, white,
Pink, gold flowers and budding trees.
Hungry children camp by night
In playgrounds. Fallen helmets bleed.
I paint the tablets of the law
Carved for passers-by to read,
Hives of honey, caves of war.

I sketch and outline, spray and splash
Poems of earth on lifeless stone.
Cleaners come with tears to wash
The law away. I watch them groan
And vandalise, then start anew.
Painted honeyeaters sing
Near orchids flowering midnight blue,
Petals and wet leaves glistening.

Seasons of Mortality

On the first morning after her betrayers
And torturers laid her torn flesh to lie
In a hollow they scooped out of grey, sliding sand
And covered her with leaves, branches, twigs,
Detritus of the whispering forest's slow
Seasons of life, flies settled to their feast.

On the second day, ants arrived on their ruthless,
Improvised, methodical highways, journeying outward
And homeward with nourishment from the recently dead.
Birds wailed and rang and rough eucalypts
Brushed the sky with clouds of fertility.
At twilight the first foxes came to plunder.

By the third day her maimed and discoloured face,
The spirit and the breath of air already forgotten,
With love's casual joy and the terror of her dying,
Spoke quietly through mulch, and bone answered,
Giving its mute account of time that dwindled
Helplessly into rain and earth and silence.

Week after week, cars travelled on the road
That lay out of reach and out of earshot, far
From the deep bush where something that once lived,
Distributed now among scavenging insects and birds,
Cats, foxes, marsupials and soil,
Offered its story to oblivion and the sun.

Then summer came again and grey leaves baked,
Hung and slept on their boughs, barely moving
In the swollen air. New generations of small,
Instinctual life pursued their allotted trails,
Insect, rat, snake, lizard, carnivore,
Foraging, gathering, killing with hot teeth.

The seventh month, lightning scarred the forest.
Fire caught and explored doomed leaves. Flame towered
Above dying branches and soared over veiled hills
And through curtains of darkness. Decades' undergrowth
Withered to bare, black ground, and charred limbs
Lay camouflaged among cinders and wells of smoke.

The seasons turned and winter floods bathed earth's
Burned heritage. The peace of spring restored
Stately, blackened trunks with soft greenery,
Filled damaged gullies with gentle swaths of grass,
And fields of blue, velvet and crimson starlight
And miniature banners cascaded over rocks and bones.

Death of a Novelist

The last chapter arrives through my open windows.
Light begins, falters, emerges and spreads
Over stoic treetops, vegetable beds,
Grass and the narrow creek where bamboo grows.
My heart pauses, throbs, races and slows.
How dazzlingly the end of hours runs!
My characters surround my bed with banners,
Sky-blue satin, fierce golds and reds
Glowing like a field of wildflowers in the sun's
Dawn welcoming peace with delicate colours.

These banners flutter with histories. I read
In the hands of my first heroine, now grown grey,
How I sent her to battle terrorists far away
In an enemy's uniform, suffer alone and bleed,
Kill and interrogate to meet my imagined need.
Blood streams down the fabric, staining her arms.
A father and mother I invented out of shame
Turn from their wounded children and wander astray.
Their road passes over rivers and barren farms.
Breeze from my window ripples their embroidered name,

Looped into pennants like silver. A slim, rejected
Child holds a tapestry of murder,
Pink blood, red wounds, white flesh and a stitched border
Of chrysanthemums. A policeman shows dejected
Houses, violent streets. Roses, perfected
By hours of gentle labour, leaven the garden
I gave him. Illiterate lovers who fought to the end
Reproach me with their dying and the prurient reader.
They carry tear-stained flags bestowing pardon.
Light sparkles from the creek and branches bend.

My first, controlling fiction was that God
Is only rogues' pretending, brigands' thieving.
Around my crimson quilt my unbelieving
Characters with their flaring streamers trod.
But now the herald lifts the flowering rod.
Trumpets announce the coming of strange light.
My poor creations fade. Their memories, sewn,
Dyed and painted, fall. I watch them leaving,
The present passing. Bamboo, day and night
Crumble. The herald beckons. I answer alone.

The Three Gardens

Far past the slowly rising, peaceful farms,
The rocks and meadows, into matted bush
I followed a gravel track amid the crush
Of vines and shrubs, orchids the sun warms,
Damp clay it never touches. Walking now,
My car left on the shoulder, I crossed the brow
Of a rough hill, battered by winter storms
Past memory, and nourished by cool shade.
I came, as he'd told me, where the water played

Around shining boulders and a deep pool spread
Where the valley fell in its majesty of ferns.
There a field of white flowers bends and turns.
This is the garden of the homeless dead.
A thousand different blooms, rose, amaryllis,
Daisy, agapanthus, clematis,
Almond blossom, delicate tropical orchid,
Each pure white, like a snowdrift, like a bride.
All held the memory of lost souls who had died

Alone, unfriended. White in spite of kind,
A child's hand, an old man's drunken dream,
A young girl's abandonment, flowering in a stream
Of white stalks and petals. What I came to find,
I found here among marigold, camellia,
Chrysanthemum, boronia, bougainvillea,
Riddling in the valley. Then the way declined
More steeply, winding past twined, tangled wood
To a field of crimson flowers, red like the blood

Of a million orphans pouring over dazzling sand.
This was the garden of the dead in war.
Rich general, mercenary, captain, poor,
Unwilling conscript, soldier proud to stand
For centuries of faith and civilisation,
Grew in death to soft, flowering crimson.
No need to name the flowers. Wild, unplanned,
They wave forever in the shelter of the wind,
The rain, the morning. But here the trees thinned,

Grey, grainy soil met me, and the last
Flourishing of anguished memory chilled the air.
Here is the garden of the dead in despair.
Black flowers, black lilies hold the past
And its sharp leaves of tragedy, and dry
Sand lies around the voiceless many who die
Uncomforted. Black amaranth, sound and taste
Of nameless grief remembered always, never,
Wrens dancing, and the whispering of the river.

Father and Child

I had a dream that spoke to me of thousands
Of families broken, suffering. A man
Journeyed on the foreshore with a child, their hands
Linked and gently swaying. Ripples ran,
Leaving draggled weeds, fish, jellyfish dead
On the yellow shore. The man paused to spread
Comforting cream on the deep, angry scars
That marred the boy's back. When father and son
Resumed their steps, it seemed a thousand million
Shadows of sons, mothers, fathers, daughters,
Broken by something none could understand,
Danced around them over the stained sand
In measures of unkindness, parents cursing their partners,
Apparitions in tumult on the furrowed waters.

VII

A young and troubled century

The Pioneers' Dream

1

We raised our camp and piled our provisions
Beside a dry, white lake
Surrounded by spinifex and stoic grass
In search of lands where budding cities could take
Or farms seed crops to feed the earthly mind,
Explorers of the bare, unfriendly
Shores and rough, unintelligible lands
In the year of mercy eighteen twenty-three.
We watched the stars pass
Into mountainous weather and felt drizzle begin,
Lifted on the small wind,
Drizzle muttering on our tent's chilly canvas,
Friendless, comfortless gestures of faint sound.
Animals rustled, sighed, groaned
And the sky whistled.
We slept and dreamed our dreams and we saw visions.

2

The mirage of a city marched ahead.
Tall, passionless buildings, ablaze
With sheer glass, threw back the sun.
Gangs of bereaved young people, bewildered, raw,
Deprived of hope and family told riddles
Of misery. Their future lay dying
On casual street corners, and suffering.
Broken families sent them on their path
To prison cells and robberies,
Ignorance of the fire and histories
Of anguish, ignorance of word and time.
Mazes of light made labyrinths of death.
Blithe faces chatted in bright cafés.
Then the day sent its summoning
Arms out of swollen clouds and awoke the sand.
We moistened our mouths with water, and ate bread.

3

And we saw those visions anew, the morning's anger.
Towering windows blazed with merchandise,
Shouted cruel inanities like murder.
Mother and father, neighbour,
Parent and child, lover,
Consumed by bitterness, parted, burned
In silent anguish and unspoken hate,
Crushed by staggering burdens of defeat.
Spinifex seemed to shudder under the weight
Of children tramping the homeless street
That veiled the salty lake.
A million torn souls wailed to escape
From mechanical oceans waiting for lights to break.
Grey grasses whispered the city's rape.
Then painfully our own year returned.
Nineteenth century rain, cloud, hunger.

4

We met strange times no thought could understand.
Pioneers from a young and troubled century
Of intellectual passion and exploration,
Cruel prisons, ships and poverty,
Faithful, hopeful journeying towards a new world,
We watched a future Dark Age flower
Through gardens of trivial, unendurable light.
We who carry Shakespeare's poems and plays,
The Bible and the living essays of Addison
In our canvas packs to help us when long days
Dwindle into the darkness of the plains
Observed the terrible blackness of a shining mansion
Bare of books and faith. And we who endure the pains
Of aching limbs and feet and scanty provender,
The morning's wearisome heat, the slow night's cold,
Saw shattered families dancing on wet sand.

5

We witnessed the gentleness and mercy of the courageous
Who recognized the tragedy in their midst,
Saw men and women visiting the young
Unparented and moving willingly among
The damaged floors and furniture of years,
Scars of illiteracy and thin addicts
Gathering ghosts of comfort where they might.
We saw them take young orphans by their arms
And help them find new strength, help injured soldiers
Conscripted to sad wars under cold sunlight
Fight to wake and touch the sun with trust.
We that wander looking for good farms
From lakes to pastures, river to changeable sea,
For land to rear towns in the still, white dust,
Heard spirits in prison laugh to be set free,
Found artistry of love in the fire of ages.

In the Cathedral of the Homeless

At the end of a long sermon the old preacher
Paused and looked around his congregation
(And yet they belonged not to him but another)
And said: Let me talk for a moment about compassion,
Suffering with the lost and damaged as with our own
Lost loves, our turbulence through sleepless
Hours, loneliness in the morning. This alone,
It may be, teaches us to see light in the homeless
Countenance, young man or woman on the hard
Concrete of their fractured families, lives,
To know that they are only ourselves, not tarred
And branded strangers, and so hope survives.

God doesn't suffer, so our theologians
Teach us, being omnipotent and wise.
But still, in hostels, needle exchanges, prisons,
I've seen Christ gazing at me through young eyes
Bewildered by the world in which they've woken
To daily nightmares, cataclysmic theft
Of all their small possessions. Visions broken
On rocks of ruined heritage, what's left
But humble, kindly gestures, grasp of a hand?
I've seen calm evil in the old face of a sadist,
Love in a victim, battled to understand
The daily breath of friendship, courtesy, trust.

And sometimes it's seemed to me that infinite wisdom
Must suffer with the agonies of his creatures,
Watching the shame we make from our gift of freedom,
Ignorant of its power and its terrors,
To strike death from atoms, to maim the stolen,
To deny itself through sterile philosophy,
To rob the injured in the name of false words spoken.
May we not pity God who has to see
The harrowed spirits we meet all around us
Struggling in their silence? How should Christ not cry
Once again in the agony of the cross,
To know lost sheep embrace blind wolves that die?

I'm no theologian. I flounder among these
And other subtle mysteries, find no shore
Of certainty among the chopping seas
Of thought, experience, language, terror and war,
Homelessness and happiness. Only one
Island in that ocean's endless dream,
That Christ, by whom all things made and begun
And ended have their lives, came into the stream
Of human joy and misery till he bled
And cried out. He taught us each lost spirit,
Even yours, even the homeless and unfed,
Is an unsurpassable flame awake with light

That we must cherish. The old man faltered, bowed
His head. If all these things are true, he whispered
Softly. They saw the joy that sang aloud
Around his thinning hair, the shock he'd suffered
For others and himself. They saw his ageing
Hands, his lined mouth, burden of memory
Low on his shoulders, rich emotion raging
In the deep places of his long years, quietly,
Unobtrusively, burden of the struggle
For signs of harmony. The secret chorus
Of unseen homeless voices filled the cathedral,
Chanted its thanks, and touched his brow with grace.

Easter Saturday

The world was calm; it rested; the savage hills,
Impassive streets and parks seemed to question,
Houses with their doors closed and laneways
Where rough grass sprouted in tired shadows
That spread invisibly toward evening, the quiet roads
Waiting helplessly to receive the loud night's traffic,
Seemed to wonder what they had done, as day
Drew out its emptiness, faded to reproachful twilight.
And after his death, Christ descended into hell,
And hunted for souls among the seared and broken.

He came to the hells of Northbridge, where
He met a child who watched his mother
Injecting heroin, crouched in a corner,
A dingy corner of a dingy square.
Her hair fell onto a rusty table
Left by a restaurant long closed.
Dreams clouded her sight. She dozed
Under matted hair, blind, pitiable.

Easter Saturday. Lights began to flash,
Music drummed electronically and screamed.
Parties got under way and the dull bass boomed
While he travelled into the hells of cold.

He rose in an ill-smelling lift
That creaked wearily, to the twelfth floor
And found, behind a narrow door
Among the smells of meals left
Around a mouldering kitchen sink
To moulder many weeks ago,
A father shedding stupid, slow
Tears over an empty drink,
His daughter crying in her sea
Of loneliness and misery,
Her TV singing mockingly.

Evening's discretion stretched across rural fields.
Tangled, gnarled barbed wire shrank into glimpsed
Ageing metal sparkling in the tenuous light,
Strung around washed fence posts and sharp bushes
That jabbed at the deepening greyness like clustered knives.
Cattle retired placidly to wordless dreams
And he carried gentle truth to the hells of hate.

'Girls are good for only one thing,'
Wounded voices snarled, and so
They threw her to the verge below
Their panelled, painted, over-revving
Van that faded into sorrows,
Faded into the street's nightmare.
Torn and bloodstained, unaware
Of where or what she was, she rose,
Wondered where to go, that hour
Of pain and solitary terror.

Blackness spread and cooled the dreaming ocean,
But silver danced in uncountable cold ripples,
Small waves swelling, clashing and falling like mountains,
Miniature, endless, complex ranges of shifting,
Shuddering black water and hidden life
Darting, sailing, staring, quarrelling like armies
Of mountaineers and miners in valleys of winter,
Hannibal's mad armies in changeable Alps,
Pharaoh's troops rolling under galloping tides.
Silver shadows moved across the water.
He hunted for shipwrecked friends in the hells of pain.

A terraced, plastered house on a lavish,
Glimmering road. Bright music pattered.
Desperate women yawned and chattered,
Waiting to deal their youth for cash
Or credit card to strangers' leers,
Lowered mouths and raised arms,
Lined eyes and transient names,
Familiar faces, old men's tears.

Partygoers shouted and fighters fought.
Branches rustled and shone in the shivering bush.
Easter Saturday sank toward its midnight.
These and many others he gathered and led
To meet him with his saints and chosen prophets,
The faithful thief who turned to him while dying,
The condemned who saw his face in his final shame,
Guided them to the gates of restoration,
Slow paths of mending and long recovery,
To walk with him and touch the timeless lakes
That heal and the walls of Paradise.

Saturday Evening, Sunday Morning

in memory of Associate Professor Ann Galloway

How can I praise the dead in a drowning country?
Harsh with disillusion, evening's long
Disharmony of loud, discordant song
Begins, and roars of animality
Float on warm winds. Drug dealers climb stairs
Downward to hell, and brutal music pounds
The memory of thought's lost, reverent grounds.
But recollection takes me unawares,
The schools we visited, the planes we'd ride,
Your faith, how much too soon you suffered, died.

Each human animal has the chance to plunge
Below the placid beasts, to bellow words
Of shame, more dumb of meaning than the birds
That cry in flocks on swaying trees; to lunge
At self and sex and screen, at screen and sex,
And know the less, the more their certainty,
Or to endeavour strenuous paths and see
The spreading sun. But roads are strewn with wrecks,
Broken windows shatter and fall like showers
Of rain troubling the madness of late hours.

These are my bitter thoughts, not yours. Researcher,
You travelled thousands of miles to study schools,
In government departments strove with fools,
Time-servers and the ignorant. Principal, teacher
And pupil made you welcome in the red
Deserts and green suburbs. With chocolate cake,
You won the heart of staff rooms, learned to take
Wisdom from words the disenfranchised said.
Woman of faith, when a hard, wasting disease
Wracked you with loss, communion gave grace.

This much I saw of you. But what we know
Of one another is a glimpse of sand
On the surface of deep mines; or, where trees stand
And brush the clouds with leaves that drift and flow
Through centuries, a snapshot of a moment.
Deride your faith or work who will, they prove
The superficial puddles where they move
And spend their being, scrabbling in the distant
Shallows while slow tides of suffering shake
The ocean, and the reefs crumble and break.

It may be that the world sinks always further
Into its night, the darkness it has chosen,
Fostered and inflicted on its children,
Breaking their homes and families till they'd rather
Drowse in front of screens than read and live,
Dance to songs that thud and wail with rage
Than know the dawning sun, the flowering page.
Patiently you worked with seeds that give
Hope in the shadows, nourish the young to turn
From needle and stolen car, to change and learn.

The long night and its violence pass. Now Sunday
Morning brings me to church, and on the wall
Above the altar, one who bled for all
Who trust him, all who falter on the way,
Since each must fail, holds out sculpted palms
In agonies of love to traitor, saint,
Time-server, betrayed child, writhing patient,
Late-comer to the feast. Your memory calms
My bleak, unending wars. Too early dead,
You comfort me. The priest prepares the bread.

VIII

The last judgement

The Last Judgement of the Homeless

Across the fields and through a rutted gate,
Over the stream where gentle bushes flower
Red and gold, and eucalypts lean and wait
For the brook to flood, their leaves brushing the water,
The chapel of the homeless stands.
In devastating art behind the altar,
Painted bodies tower as light commands.

Cattle peer through open windows. Ravens'
Creaking music sounds in the rush of air
Through distant leaves, and the brook's turbulence
Crossing rocks and roots. The pews are bare
And polished, and the stained glass
Catches shafts of light from the painting, where
They dance around the chapel and dust-motes pass.

The unimaginable features of the one
Last judge, imagined somehow and portrayed,
Are gathered in the warm light of the sun,
A new sun, pouring fire, dispelling shade.
This is the face of love, at once
Stern and kind, by whom all things were made,
Incarnate truth and fateful Providence.

Thrown by the fury of heaven's clear light
Showing their secret hearts, lost bodies fall
Through dazzling space. One hides in vain the sight
Of writhing darkness, one who heard the call
To help a starving, desperate child
And closed his ears and pledged himself to all
The pettiness of days his hands defiled.

Charon, the weary boatman, lifts his oar
Menacingly, and his gleaming eye
Subdues the bureaucrat who would ignore
The street where every day young people die.
He nurtured his career for this,
To sail to dreary worlds of agony,
Forever dwindling, lost from morning's bliss.

Dwindling forever, but something still endures,
A shadow of disgrace, a thought of hate
In the squandered flesh that walks the joyless shores,
The rocks of emptiness. Thoughts dissipate.
Minos and his lowering stare
Consign the cruel and negligent to the state
They chose for others; demons drag them there.

Here are the gangsters, here the gang that raped,
Laughing and sneering; then, imprisoned, further
Victims groaned beneath them. None escaped,
And nor shall these escape. See how they cover
Ears against the frightful sound
Of judgement ringing. These two committed murder
Before their child's face, wrecked holy ground.

And far beyond them, out of reach of ignorance
Self-condemned to torment, in the clear
Open blue of heaven, saints advance,
Remembering past suffering. They come near,
Observe God's peaceful, angry brow,
And lift eternal hands in holy fear.
These are the homeless, housed forever now.

A child of cold night and the streets, whose birth
Began a long catastrophe of laws
And cruelty, remorseless until death
Released her, reaches down past cloud and draws
A woman who once showed her grace
Into the light of heaven that grows and soars
Like joy awakening on a lover's face.

With signs of martyrdom they met in life,
They face the judge; the needle, the barbed wire.
One holds a rifle, one a jagged knife,
Portrait of a parent's face hot with desire
Or rage. Each gave another food
When she was hungry. Here they form the choir
That shares the forgiveness of the bloodstained wood.

'Let me cleanse the murk out of your eyes,'
Saved angels whisper. They are like the dawn
Spreading over a grey lake; like sunrise
Lightening shadowy hills. And young men, torn
And traumatised by years in jail,
Move anxious looks towards the infinite ocean
Of life, the living hope that will not fail.

The mother of the judge turns from her son
To sad reflection. Dressed in green and red,
She ponders deadly mysteries begun
In a small room centuries ago. Around her head,
Radiances of creation speak.
A white scarf and her son's robe join in painted
Harmony. Her young hands touch her cheek.

Arches open on remoter schools of time
Unfolding to eternity. Light swerves
Across the pews, and doglike shadows climb
White marble walls. A small gold flower curves
And dances in the mounting day.
Dappled black and pale, a cow observes
The parable of love and judgement's play.

Few come past the chapel. Fewer see
The passionate art that flows on its painted wall,
The raised arm of the judge, the misery
Of self-maimed souls that shrivel as they fall,
The flash of trumpets summoning
Time to its morning, or the judge's call
To street children for their last long welcoming.

The fields spread and quiet water strays
Between reeds and branches. White pillars of heaven
Tower into the sky and find the day's
Music that lights grey clouds. The cawing raven
Thrusts its beak into vacancy,
Utters its desperate voice. What the painter has given
Lives on rough stone in promise of endless mercy.

Now and tomorrow death and violence
Rule city, field and farm, scar barren street.
I saw this chapel long ago with once
Familiar friends. Where burning instants meet
The pain of history's despair,
The hand of judgement makes the sky complete
And art draws heaven's peace from singing air.

www.ingramcontent.com/pod-product-compliance
Lightning Source LLC
Chambersburg PA
CBHW070909080526
44589CB00013B/1232